HOW TO PLAY

CRICKET

HOW TO PLAY

CRICKET

PETER
RICE

GUINNESS

Published by Guinness Books
33 London Road
Enfield
Middlesex EN2 6DJ

Produced and Designed by Mander Gooch Callow

Illustration: Sharon F. Gower

Printed and bound in Great Britain by
Hazell Watson & Viney Ltd., Aylesbury

British Library Cataloguing in Publication Data

  Rice, Peter
    How to play cricket.
    1. Cricket – Manuals
    1. Title
    796.35'82

ISBN 0-85112-371-6

Contents

Basics of Batting

All cricketers enjoy batting but to be successful, it is essential to have a sound technique. Some cricketers are born with a natural gift for timing and a 'good eye'. The styles of great batsmen may vary, but almost all adhere to the basic principles of good batting. Less naturally talented players can become good batsmen with hard practice at these same basic principles.

Every player, whatever his natural ability should be aware of his limitations as well as his strengths. Your strengths are enhanced by the correct techniques acquired playing particular scoring strokes, based on sound defence. If your technique is at fault, then your limitations will be exposed.

Whilst all batsmen are looking to score off every ball, this is not always possible and the need to defend the good ball is just as important.

The ideal place to develop sound technique is in the nets. The decision whether to play on the front or back foot, the correct movement of head, body, feet and bat as soon as the ball is delivered, will all become instinctive with practice. A good batsman will concentrate, watch the ball closely, keep still and ensure that his top hand controls all straight bat strokes.

Before you even begin to think about stroke technique you need to master the correct grip, stance and backlift.

The Grip

(Right-hand, left- hand opposite)

If you are going to hit the ball with full force, whether it is pitched on the off-side or leg-side of the wicket, the grip is very important.

To establish the correct grip, lay the bat face down on the floor, with the handle pointing towards you. Bend down and grip the bat handle approximately halfway down with your right hand and pick it up as if picking up an axe.

Without releasing the grip, bring your left hand into contact with the top of the handle. Both hands should be as near to the top of the handle as possible, to prevent restriction of movement. Your fingers and thumbs should be well round the handle, with the top hand gripping firmly.

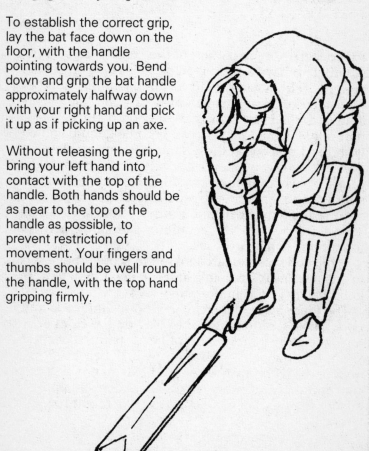

Bring the bat to rest against your front pad with the 'V' between your forefinger and thumb on both hands, in line down the handle, at a position mid-point between the face of the bat and middle, with the back of your top hand, facing approximately towards mid-off.

FAULT-FINDER

If your hands are too far apart, with your right hand too low down the handle, they won't work together as they should for all straight bat strokes. It will also result in your right hand taking over the shot, with a tendency to play across the line. If the back of your left hand is behind the handle, the stroke will be restricted.

The Stance

The correct stance will allow you to move on to the front or back foot easily.

Your feet should be about 6" apart, either side of and parallel to, the batting crease. Both knees should be slightly bent, with your weight distributed evenly between each foot. This allows an easier movement forwards or backwards. Your body should be sideways on, with your head and left shoulder pointing down the wicket towards the bowler. Your head should remain upright and your eyes level with the pitch. The base of the bat should be placed just behind your back foot, with the face pointing towards your front leg.

FAULT-FINDER

If your feet are too far apart, your initial movement will be impeded. If your stance is too open, the result will be incorrect backlift and it will make it difficult to lead into straight bat strokes on the off-side, with your left shoulder and head. If your head leans too far over to the off-side, you could lose your balance and if you don't keep your eyes level, you may get a distorted view of the delivery of the ball.

LAW-BREAKER

When you take up position at the wicket, make sure that you are in your ground. You or the bat in your hand must be behind the line of the popping crease. You can be stumped or run out if you are outside your ground in certain circumstances.

THE UMPIRE'S DECISION
Out

The Backlift

The next important basic of technique is the backlift. Remember the straighter the backlift, the greater the chance of playing a straight stroke.

With your eyes on the direction from which the ball is coming, draw the bat backwards and upwards, making sure that your left forearm is in line with the face of the bat. Your elbows should be clear of your body, with your right wrist higher than the elbow. Continue the backlift until the bat is shoulder-height and the face of the bat is pointing out to point position. Your head and body should be balanced and still.

LAW-BREAKER
If you haven't touched the ball with your bat, beware of coming between a fair ball which would have hit the wicket and the wicket. If you touch it with any part of you, your clothes or equipment, you will be out LBW.
There is room for appeal because the ball must be pitched in a straight line between the wickets or on the off-side of your wicket.

The point of impact needn't be below the level of the bails, but it must be in a straight line between the wickets.

THE UMPIRE'S DECISION
Out
If he thinks you have not tried to play the ball the umpire can still call you out LBW, even if you are outside the line of the off-stump when you intercept.

It is important to let your top hand control the backlift and keep your right wrist higher than the elbow to ensure that the face of the bat opens.

Once the basic grip, stance and backlift have been mastered, you can proceed to the various batting strokes, both attacking and defensive, which all start from this basic position.

LAW-BREAKER
Don't dawdle on to the pitch if you are next in the batting order. You have two minutes from the moment the wicket falls, to step on to the field, or you might suffer the indignity of being OUT TIMED OUT.

THE UMPIRE'S DECISION
When he is appealed to, the umpire at the bowler's end would have to decide whether you were dawdling deliberately or not, so there is some discretion if you are unavoidably delayed.

Forward Strokes

Forward defensive strokes

This type of shot is played to a good length, straight ball.

You begin the backlift when the bowler is in his delivery stride. As the ball is delivered, lean forward, with your left shoulder and head moving into the line of the ball. With this movement, the balance of your body and left foot will follow your shoulder automatically.

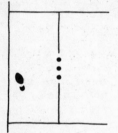

Your left foot moves at right-angles to your right foot, with your back foot anchored behind the batting crease.

At this point your left knee and shoulder should be in front of your left foot and your head directly over it. Bring the bat down in line with your front leg, not allowing any daylight between bat and pad. Keep your left elbow as high as possible and relax the grip of your bottom hand into a pencil grip of forefinger and thumb, so as not to allow too much power in the shot. Your back foot remains still to maintain your balance.

FAULT-FINDER

1. Are you leading with your head and left shoulder?
2. Are you bending your left knee?
3. Make sure you are taking your left foot far enough forward.
4. Keep your back foot anchored.
5. Make your left hand controls the shot.
6. Are you keeping the full face of the bat along the line of the ball?

Attacking forward strokes

Most attacking forward strokes (drives) are very productive scoring shots and you should be always looking for the half volley to use the drive. A sound technique and the ability to hit down the line of the ball are essential to the drives.

The straight drive

The straight drive is played to a straight delivery, pitched well up to the batsman on the line of the stumps and hit on the half-volley, between the bowler and mid-off. The stroke begins with the same grip and stance as the forward defence.

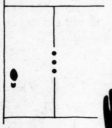

LAW-BREAKER
Once you have played your stroke, you can only strike the ball twice if you are guarding your wicket. This includes striking the ball with any part of you and the batting hand is considered to be part of the bat in this case. If the other side appeals to the umpire, he could decide that you are OUT HIT THE BALL TWICE. Don't hit the ball back to a fielder either unless you have permission from the other side.

THE UMPIRE'S DECISION
He would have to decide whether you hit the ball twice on purpose. He would also be looking out for a case of obstructing the ball from being caught. You can be out on these grounds if you are in the way of a throw-in, even if you are guarding your wicket. It is small consolation that the bowler won't be credited with the wicket. In any case if he decides that the ball was legitimately hit twice you can't score any runs from this ball.

Draw the bat up into the backlift on the path of the ball, with your left arm close to your body. On the downswing, move your right arm close to your body, as your left foot and left shoulder lean forwards, towards the bowler. Your left foot is at the side of the pitch of the ball, with your left knee bent. Your weight is over your front leg and your back foot is anchored.

Contact with the ball is made close to your front foot, with your head well over the ball. Keep your left elbow high and push through with your right hand, following through the line of the ball, in the direction the ball is to be hit, until your bat is at about shoulder-height.

The off drive

The off drive is played to a delivery that is slightly over-pitched, just outside off-stump.

The shot begins with a full backlift with the bat face opened. Your head and left shoulder lead in the direction of the shot and your foot is as near to the pitch of the ball as possible, pointing towards extra-cover. Your weight is on your front foot with your left knee bent.

Bring the bat down, with your top hand controlling the stroke, to make contact with the ball as close to your front foot as possible. Let the heel of your back foot rise, but don't allow your foot to pivot.

The bat must follow through the line of the shot being played.

Your head should remain in position over your front foot. Don't allow it to come up too early.

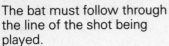

LAW-BREAKER
Be careful not to touch the ball in play with your non-batting hand, this applies to both batsmen. If the other side appeals you could be OUT HANDLED THE BALL.

THE UMPIRE'S DECISION
The umpire would have to decide whether the ball was handled on purpose before he says that you are out. If this is his decision, the bowler won't get the credit for the wicket.

The check drive

The check drive is played very much like the off drive, except that the follow-through is checked, rather than carried through over your left shoulder.

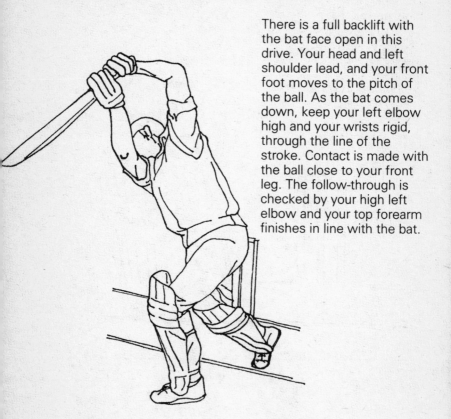

There is a full backlift with the bat face open in this drive. Your head and left shoulder lead, and your front foot moves to the pitch of the ball. As the bat comes down, keep your left elbow high and your wrists rigid, through the line of the stroke. Contact is made with the ball close to your front leg. The follow-through is checked by your high left elbow and your top forearm finishes in line with the bat.

FAULT-FINDER

If you move your head, you could lose balance, resulting in your playing across the line and lifting the ball in the air.

The cover drive
The cover drive is played to a delivery that is slightly over-pitched outside the off-stump.

The execution is very much the same as that of the off drive, except that your front foot goes further across towards the off-side. This means that the ball is hit through the cover area on the half volley.

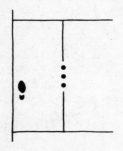

LAW-BREAKER
If you play the ball, off the bat (or the hand or wrist holding the bat) and a fielder catches and holds it before it touches the ground, you will be OUT CAUGHT.

THE UMPIRE'S DECISION
Out

The on drive

The on drive is played to a ball pitched well up to the batsman, just outside leg-stump.

You play this shot very much like the off drive but with the ball pitched on the leg-side. Your left foot and shoulder lead, but open slightly to allow your head to lead on to the line of the stroke. At the pitch of the ball, your front foot is just outside leg-stump.

Draw the bat down in a long, flat swing, dipping your left shoulder slightly. The face of the bat makes contact with the ball as square to the line of the stroke as possible. The ball is driven hard past mid-on. The stroke is completed with the bat following through the line of the shot and over your front shoulder.

Keep your head still throughout the shot, so that there is no falling away to the off-side.

The lofted drive

When you play the lofted drive, contact with the ball is made slightly sooner than in drives along the ground and at a point in front of your front foot.

Although still leading with your head, keep it slightly behind the ball at the moment of contact. Let your body come up slightly as you hit the ball. Swing through in the direction of the ball with your arms (hands leading) and full extension. Your front foot should be pointing towards mid-off.

Moving out to drive

To make a slower, good length ball into one which can be driven, you can move out to drive.

Draw the bat up, into a high backlift. Your head and left shoulder still lead, with your left arm in control. As your weight moves on to your left foot, your right foot moves up behind it and keeps your body sideways. Your head and left shoulder lead into the stroke.

If you move your feet correctly, you should reach the pitch of the ball just outside off-stump. From this point, use the same technique as for the other drives. Keep the swing as low as possible to make contact with the ball, with the face of the bat square to the line of the shot.

Your weight should be all on your front foot now, with your head leading. Your arms follow through in an arc over your left shoulder, after the ball has been hit through the off-side.

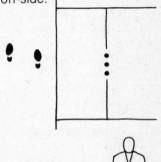

LAW-BREAKER
You are never safe from the wicket keeper. Remember the crease belongs to him. If you move out of your ground, unless you are going for a run and the ball was not a 'no ball' he will stump you. That is as long as the ball hasn't been touched by a fielder.

THE UMPIRE'S DECISION
The wicket keeper doesn't have to actually throw the ball, it can bounce off him or his clothes or be kicked at the wicket and you would still be stumped. If however, he stumps you from in front of the wicket when the ball has not touched either you or your bat, you are not stumped.

Leg glance (front foot)

Ideally, the front foot leg glance should be played to a good length ball, that is pitched on or just outside the line of your pads.

The technique is very much the same as for the forward defensive shot, in that the bat is drawn up into the backlift position and your head and left shoulder lead into the shot.

Move your front foot forwards, to land just inside the line of the ball. Your hands lead in front of the bat, so that the ball is played down. Contact with the ball is made just in front of your front pad with your wrists turning the face of the bat towards the leg-side. After contact, keep your head and body in front of your front leg with your head down. Don't let your body fall away towards the off-side.

The sweep
The sweep shot is played to a good length ball, pitched outside leg-stump from a slow bowler.

Draw the bat up into a high backlift position. Keep your head square and your eyes level. Lean forward with your left shoulder and move your left foot forwards to the pitch of the ball, with your foot pointing down the wicket.

Push forwards, to bend your left leg fully.

Keep your right foot firmly anchored, and bring the bat down, with your arms straight, in an arc and 'sweep' the ball to leg, rolling your wrists to keep the ball down. Keep your head still and on the line of the ball throughout.

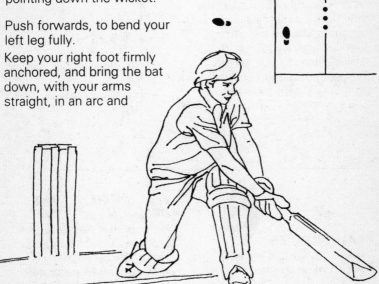

FAULT-FINDER

It is important that your front foot lands in line with with the ball, that your knees are bent and that contact is made with your arms at full stretch.

Backward Strokes

Back foot defence
This shot is played to a delivery just short of a length, pitched on middle or middle and off-stump.

Adopt the normal stance and as the ball is delivered, draw the bat into the backlift position. As the ball pitches, moves your right foot backwards, parallel to the popping or batting crease, but in line with the ball.

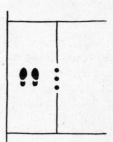

LAW-BREAKER
If you break the wicket when making your stroke, or as you get ready to do so, or even as you prepare to run or having played the ball are off on your first run, you can be OUT HIT WICKET. It doesn't matter whether the wicket is hit with your bat, your body or clothes -you are still out.

THE UMPIRE'S DECISION
He could decide that you are not out, if he believes that the wicket was hit while you were actually running or to avoid being stumped or run out. Also if you are trying to avoid a throw-in or, if the bowler doesn't deliver the ball after he has started his run-up or action.(He would signal 'DEAD BALL' in this last case.

You must make sure that your back foot is parallel to the crease, to allow your body to remain sideways. The backlift and left elbow should be as high as possible to allow the ball to be played down. Your left hand should control the bat to make sure that the bat face is kept on the line of the ball. You must also make sure that your bottom hand relaxes the grip.

Bring the bat downwards, keeping your left elbow as high as possible. Your forearm is in line with the face of the bat. At the same time, move your left foot back towards your right. The bat continues downwards, as you relax the grip of your bottom hand to pencil grip (thumb and forefinger). Keep the bat close to your body and angle back from the handle to the base of the stumps.

Your head should be looking down the line of the ball, to ensure that the ball is played down. There is no follow-through with this shot.

Backward leg glance

The backward leg glance is played to a delivery just short of a length and which is going to miss leg-stump. It is played to run the ball down to long-leg.

Draw the bat up into a high backlift position and as the ball pitches, move your right foot back towards the stumps, with your toes pointing out to cover position. Keep your weight slightly forwards as you draw your front foot backwards, to just inside the line of delivery. Then bring the bat down close to your body, keeping your left elbow high.

Your left hand is in control of the shot, with the handle just forward of the face of the bat, to angle the bat slightly backwards, so that you can play the ball downwards. As you make contact with the ball, your wrists turn, to deflect it in the required direction.

As you turn your wrists, your left elbow will drop slightly. Keep your head over the line of the ball.

FAULT-FINDER

Remember when playing this shot to let the ball come on to the bat. At the moment of contact, your head and the top of the bat should be over the ball.

Forcing shot, off the back foot

This shot is played to a delivery that is pitched just short of a length, outside the off-stump and does not bounce above the height of the stumps.

LINE OF
SHOULDERS

From the normal stance, draw the bat up into a high backlift. Then, turning your left shoulder in the direction of mid-off, move your right foot backwards, towards the stumps, in line with the ball. Your foot should come down parallel to the popping crease. Keep your head down and in front of your body, as you bring your left foot back towards your right, which is taking your weight.

Bring the bat down, with your left hand in control and your left elbow in a high position, through the line of the shot. As the bat makes contact with the ball, your right hand punches through to give power to the shot, playing the ball through the cover or extra cover area. The bat follows through very much as for the checked drive, with your left elbow still in high position and your left forearm in line with the face of the bat.

When playing this shot, you must make sure that your back foot moves far enough back and in line with the delivery. Keep your body sideways to the line of the stroke and your head forwards when making contact with the ball. Keep your left elbow high.

Pull shot

The pull shot is played to a ball pitched short of a length, at a height between waist and shoulders, on the line of the stumps.

From the normal stance, take the bat back into a high backlift position. Step back towards the stumps with your back foot, while you move your front foot backwards, level with your back foot. Your front foot should be pointing in the direction of mid-on and your back foot towards mid-off.

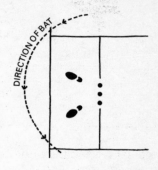

By this movement, your body will rotate through 90° to a position parallel to the popping crease. At the start of the stroke, the weight of your body is on your back foot. Meanwhile, bring the bat round from the high backlift position in an arc, parallel to the ground. Keep your arms straight and your head looking down the wicket throughout the stroke. Contact with the ball is made directly in line with the centre of your body, with the face of the bat at right-angles to the ground.

As the bat follows through, transfer your weight to your front foot, keeping your arms straight. This will ensure that your wrists will roll over to leave the face of the bat pointing to the ground. It will also keep the ball down from catching positions, hitting it through the area between mid-wicket and square-leg.

The hook shot
The hook shot is played to a fast, short pitched ball, which bounces between chest and head-height.

You need a high backlift position. When the ball pitches, moves your weight quickly on to your back foot.

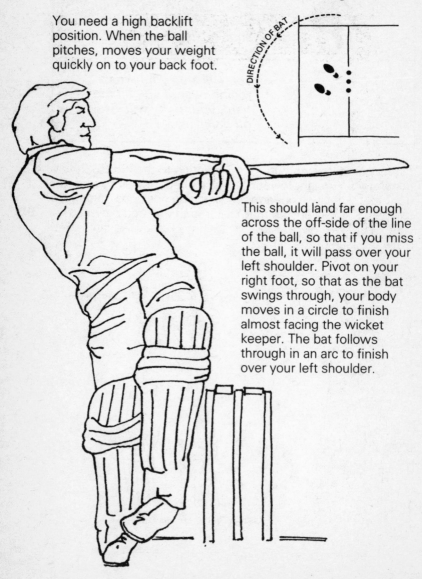

This should land far enough across the off-side of the line of the ball, so that if you miss the ball, it will pass over your left shoulder. Pivot on your right foot, so that as the bat swings through, your body moves in a circle to finish almost facing the wicket keeper. The bat follows through in an arc to finish over your left shoulder.

The square cut

The square cut is played to a ball pitched short of a length, wide of the off-stump.

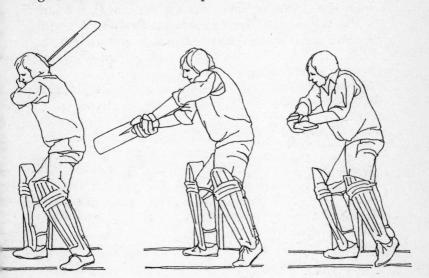

The backlift is high and as the ball pitches, you move your right foot backwards across the stumps, turning your head and left shoulder into the line of the ball. Your full weight is on your right foot and you bring the bat down with your hands thrown towards the ball, arms at full stretch. Contact with the ball is made opposite your right hip. Your right foot is facing just behind point and the ball is played down, to avoid a catch in the slips, and hit square through the off-side.

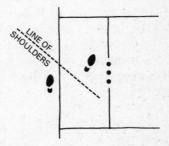

The bat follows through over your left shoulder, but you still lean your weight into the stroke.

The late cut

The late cut is played to a ball pitched short of a length, well outside off-stump.

The execution of the late cut is very much the same as the square cut. The difference is that contact with the ball is made later, as the ball is slightly wider.

To compensate for the slightly wider ball, move your back foot back, across the stumps, to land pointing towards gully. Turn your head and left shoulder further round, pointing in the direction of cover, square to your right foot. From this point, the stroke is entirely the same as the square cut, except that the ball is run down through the gully area.

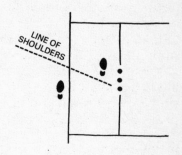

Hit to leg (full toss)

This shot is played to a full toss and it is paramount that you keep your head still and in position throughout, to prevent from swaying away on to the leg-side. As the ball does not pitch, it is important that once you pick up the line of the ball, you keep your eyes fixed on it until the completion of the shot.

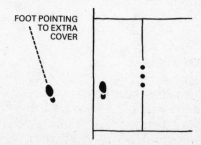

Running Between the Wickets

One of the most important principles of batting is running between the wickets. If you are alert in looking for quick singles, it could make the difference between winning and losing a match. Good calling and judgment between both batsmen is essential when running between the wickets.

Try to take the first run as quickly as possible, even if it is highly unlikely that you can score more than a single. By running and turning quickly, you may pressurize the fielder into a mis-field or a poor throw that could result in an overthrow.

When you call for a run, use as few calls as possible. The most recognised calls are YES, NO and WAIT. If you call WAIT, quickly follow this up by calling YES or NO.

You must try to get into the habit of backing up your initial call as you pass your partner while running, by saying "look for two" or "maybe three", when you have hit the ball past the in-fielders. The decision as to whether there is more than one run to be made should be left to the batsman running to the 'danger end', ie. normally the end nearest to the fielder's throw.

When you run between the wickets, change the bat from one hand to the other so that you can see the ball at all times, without having to turn or look over your shoulder.

Grounding your bat
You can cut down your actual running distance to about 16 yards if you follow this method.

Approximately one full stride from the 'popping crease', press your front foot firmly on the ground.

Bend your front knee and put the corner of the bat on

the ground and slide it along, until it is behind the 'popping crease'. At the same time, when running more than one run, turn the opposite shoulder back in the direction of the return run and push off on the front foot to complete the turn.

FAULT-FINDER

When running between the wickets the 'striker' and 'non-striker' should bear the following points in mind.

It is the responsibility of the striker to call for all runs hit in front of the wicket while the non-striker should take responsibility for all balls played behind the wicket. Of course, either batsmen can deny the run if he feels that there is a chance of being run out. His call in this instance should be a quick, decisive NO.

LAW-BREAKER
The bat must ground behind the line, not on it, as this will result in the umpire calling "one short"

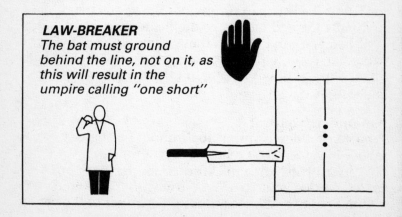

The non-striking batsman should always be backing up. This means that as the bowler runs up to bowl, the non-striking batsman should 'walk-in' with him. As the bowler reaches his delivery stride, the non-striking batsman should have reached a position on the popping crease, so that as soon as the ball has been delivered, he has moved a yard or so down the wicket on the opposite side to the bowler.

The non-striking batsman should always try to run down the same side of the wicket as he is standing, while the 'striker' should attempt to run down the side of the wicket from which the bowler has delivered the ball.

Please note that the batsmen should run down the side of the wicket and not on it.

LAW-BREAKER

Remember be careful of your ground. Either you or the batsman at the other end can be OUT RUN OUT, if you are out of your ground and the wicket is put down by the other side. That is unless you are stumped, or make good your ground or have to leave it to avoid being hurt. You can't be run out on a no-ball either, unless you have tried to score a run on it.

THE UMPIRE'S DECISION

This is sometimes a close decision and one query that often arises is which batsman is run out. The answer is that if they haven't crossed yet in their run, the batsman who has left the wicket which is put down, is out. If he returns quickly enough and the other batsman joins him at the wicket then the 2nd batsman will be out, if his wicket is put down. Incidentally, if you play the ball to the opposite wicket and it is not touched by the fielder before the wicket is put down, then you can't be run out.

Bowling

In the long history of cricket, there have been many great bowlers, each with his own action. Indeed, each and every bowler will have his natural, individual action, one which will be both comfortable and successful for him. However there are four main points which every bowler should practise, no matter how individual his style: the correct grip, the run-up, the delivery and the follow-through.

LAW-BREAKER

You are allowed to change ends during a match as often as you like as long as you don't bowl two consecutive overs in an innings.

THE UMPIRE'S DECISION

One of the umpire's decisions is to call an over. He will do this when the previously agreed number of balls (6 or 8 bowled from each wicket in turn) has been bowled, Sometimes there will be no doubt in the mind of the umpire at the bowler's end, that both sides regard the ball as out of play and he will call an over then. He will also call over when the ball is dead. He won't count either a no-ball or a wide ball as one of the over.

The Correct Grip

(Right-hand, left-hand, opposite)

Remember to hold the ball in your fingers, never in the palm of your hand.

The seam should be vertical, positioned between your first and second fingers. Note the positions of the thumb and the third finger. They are used only to support the ball from underneath.

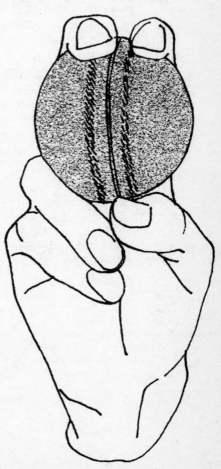

The Run-up

It is a common fault with many bowlers to use a much longer run-up than is necessary. This energy-wasting habit needs to be corrected early. The length of run-up will vary but it should be consistent with the speed at which you intend to bowl.

Once you have decided on the type of ball that you are going to bowl, you should pace out a run-up, marking its end with a white disc or similar marker. An economic run-up is one which is just long enough to allow you to accelerate smoothly from the same spot, reaching maximum speed in the final two or three strides before the bound, for each delivery.

During your run-up, you must watch the batsman for any movement. At the delivery, fix your eyes on the intended line of the ball or the spot where it is to pitch.

The Delivery

To achieve a delivery which is smooth and rhythmic throughout, a good bowler will take account of the following basic positions.

In the final stride of your run-up, bound off your left foot, turn sideways in the air, landing on your right foot, parallel to the bowling crease.

Make sure that your left shoulder is pointing down the pitch, while your body is turning sideways in the air. Your right foot passes in front of your left and turns, landing parallel to the bowling crease. You are looking down the pitch, along the intended line of the ball.

Your right foot, bearing your full weight, comes down parallel to the crease. Your left shoulder and hip are pointing down the pitch. Your back should be arched and your body leaning away from the batsman, with your knee in high position. Extend your left arm upwards, with your fingers pointing skywards. You will be looking down the pitch behind your arm. (This position is commonly known as 'the coil'.)

From the coil you move to the delivery. You start to move your right arm forwards and downwards, to start your delivery swing. Your left arm moves forwards and downwards. Your left foot begins to come down fully extended. This is the point at which you are about to transfer your weight from your right to left foot and land in line with your right leg.

At the moment of delivery your right arm is in a high position, with your left, close to your body. Your weight is now over your left foot which is absorbing the impact. You straighten your left leg, as your right leg comes forward. Your head should be over your left leg. Your left arm is thrown backwards close to your body, which has now turned square on to the batsman.

Your left arm swings well up and back and your head is still, balanced and looking down the line of the delivery. Pivot your body, bringing your right shoulder to point at the batsman. Swing your right arm down, across your braced left leg. Your right leg picks up and passes through close to your left.

The Follow-through

The follow-through consists of several strides absorbing the momentum of the bowler's action. At this stage it is important to avoid running down the pitch into the area known as the danger area. This is an area just over a metre (4 feet) from the popping crease, bounded by imaginary lines 1ft either side of the middle stump.

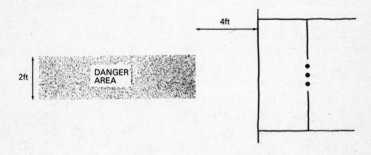

FAULT-FINDER

1. Inconsistent and non-gradual accelerating run-up.
2 Jump without sufficient height or rotation.
2. Right foot not landing parallel to the bowling crease.
3. Back not arched and insufficient lean away from the batsman.
4. Bowling off wrong foot.
5. Head not looking down the pitch from behind front arm.
6. Front foot landing too wide.
7. Not enough use of front arm.
8. Lapse of concentration. Bowler's eyes and mind not on line and length to be bowled.
9. Too long a stride will decrease the height and one that is too short will upset your balance.

Length and Direction

One of the most important qualities for a bowler, whether he be fast or slow, is to bowl a good line and length. The main aim of the fielding side is to bowl the batting side out for the least number of runs possible, so without these qualities, you will seldom be successful and a liability to your side. So what is 'line and length'?

The term 'length' is best described as the point at which the ball is pitched, in relation to the batsman's normal stance at the wicket. A good 'line' (or direction) is where the bowler should direct the ball, which in most cases will be on or just outside off-stump.

In cricket there are names given to varying lengths of delivery. The diagram shows the approximate pitching areas for the varying length of deliveries, with the batsman taking up his normal stance position.

Good length
A 'good length' is probably one of the most difficult deliveries to assess. So many factors can influence the decision. Perhaps it is best described as a ball that is pitched, to make the batsman uncertain as whether to play back or forward. Some players can determine a good length ball instinctively, others learn from hard experience. It is also true to say that what is a good length ball to one batsman, will be the opposite to another, it will depend on the build of the batsman and his reactions.

Other factors that may influence good length are whether the ball is new or old, a new ball will bounce higher than an old one for example. The state of the pitch will also have an effect, when it is slow the bowler will have to pitch the ball further up to the batsman.

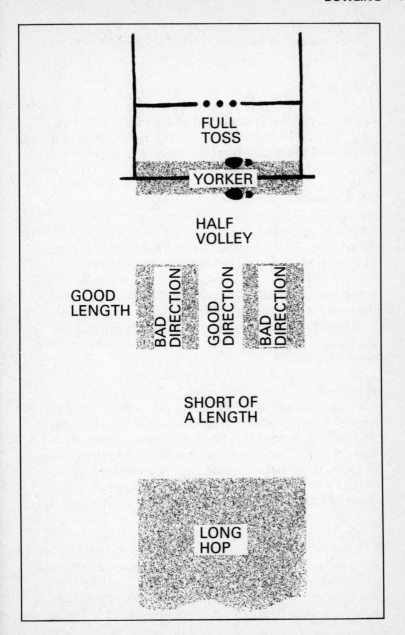

So one of the main qualities needed by a bowler is good concentration, if he is to take into account all these factors.

Long hop

The 'long hop' is a delivery that every batsman dreams of receiving and is regarded as a gift. It is pitched approximately half-way down the wicket and is devoid of pace. It is mainly pulled hard to the leg-side but can be hit anywhere in front of the wicket.

It is definitely a delivery that all bowlers should try not to bowl.

Short of a length

This is a delivery pitched nearer the batsman than the long hop and is so called because it is short of a good length. When bowled on a fast pitch, it can be a very good defensive ball, as it forces the batsman on to the back foot and does not allow him to drive the ball.

When the pitch is difficult (ie. when the ball is keeping low or lifting) this delivery can be a frequent wicket-taker.

Half volley

The 'half volley' is a ball that is pitched beyond that of a good length ball, up to the batsman. The batsman will be looking for this type of delivery, as it means he can drive the ball hard and it is a good scoring shot. But when the ball is swinging, it can be an important delivery in the attacking bowler's repertoire, as it invariably produces catches, mainly behind the wicket.

Yorker

The yorker is a delivery that all bowlers should attempt to master. It is pitched at the batsman's feet and often produces wickets when delivered with a little extra pace. When used as a surprise delivery, particularly against a new batsman, it leaves him unable to get his bat down in time to block the ball. If not bowled to perfection it can be converted easily into a half volley or full toss.

Full toss
Like the long hop, this delivery is regarded as a gift by the batsman. It does not pitch at all and reaches the batsman at varying heights. Despite its potential as a run-maker to the batsman, it can also be an effective wicket-taker, especially if the batsman mis-times his shot or when directed at the stumps, hits across the line of delivery.

Bouncer
The bouncer pitches in a similar area to the long hop, but is delivered at a fast pace, so that after pitching it lifts upwards towards the batsman's head and chest.

When used as a surprise delivery, this can be very effective for both potential wicket-taking and unnerving the batsman. It is worth pointing out that in club cricket this delivery should not be used against poor batsmen, as it can be very dangerous.

There is a feeling in cricket circles that the bouncer is used too frequently and when this happens it becomes intimidating. Umpires consider intimidation to be 'the deliberate bowling of fast, short pitched balls which by their length, height and direction are intended or likely to inflict physical injury on the batsman'.

Beamer
The beamer is a fast, full toss, delivered at head-height. Under no circumstances should a bowler attempt to bowl this delivery as it can be very dangerous to the batsman. The batsman cannot judge the pace of the ball and in some cases he never 'picks up' the ball as it leaves the bowler's hand.

In the event of such unfair bowling, the umpires will take the same action as described for the bouncer.

Fast Bowling

Genuine fast bowlers are rare and those who are medium fast should concentrate more on making the ball deviate due to swing, rather than increasing pace.

The fast bowler generally opens the bowling having first use of the new ball. Used correctly, this can be a great asset to him as the ball comes off the pitch faster and bounces higher when new.

If you are the bowler, it is most important to make the batsman play at every delivery, so as not to waste the advantage of a new ball. It is pointless for a fast bowler to keep sending in bouncers or wide balls which the batsman does not have to play. It is not only a waste of energy, it takes the shine off the new ball more quickly. The fast bowler is usually used in short bursts to maintain his maximum speed.

You should concentrate on pitching the ball on the seam, in order to obtain some movement after it has been pitched. Firstly, you need to assess the batsman's basic method of play, i.e. whether he plays off the front or back foot and make adjustments on length, to preempt his favourite stroke.

On pitches that are hard and fast, you may force the batsman to play most of his shots off the back foot and then bring in an element of surprise by firing in the occasional 'yorker'(a ball pitched at the batsman's feet). This may get through underneath the late backlift, or through a hurried defensive stroke.

Alternatively, when facing a batsman who prefers back foot strokes, you could force him to play off the front foot repeatedly and then surprise him by sending down a 'bouncer' (a ball pitched short of length to pass at chest-height), forcing him into a false stroke.

You should bowl the ball from as close to the stumps as possible, to make it more difficult for the batsman to

get to the off-side of it to attempt to hook it. It is a
major failing of bowlers attempting a bouncer, to bowl
it from wide of the crease. The result is that it will pass
harmlessly down the leg-side.

Do not overdo the use of this ball. Remember that it
is most effective when occasionally unleashed as a
surprise tactic to unsettle batsmen and make them
wary of coming on to the front foot.

Medium Bowling

The main attribute of a good, medium pace bowler is
accuracy, by maintaining good line and length on good
pitches. His ideal plan is to frustrate the batsman and
prevent him from scoring by attacking the stumps.
This strategy may force the batsman to make mistakes,
eventually getting him out when he makes a false
stroke.

As the bowler is dependent on a good length, he
must concentrate, to determine the precise spot for his
pitch.

The point at which the ball strikes the bat, in varying
conditions from day to day, will give a rough guide.
When the batsman plays forward and the bat is struck
between the shoulder and half way up, the batsman
has obviously misjudged the length. If he plays back to
a ball bouncing normally and keeps below knee-
height, he will tend to hurry his stroke because he has
mis-read a good length delivery.

If you are a medium pace bowler, you will have to
vary your tactics when the batsman is on the
defensive, e.g. when he is playing out time for a draw.
You must then set an attacking field and vary your
delivery position on the bowling crease, as well as the
pace and action, in an effort to induce mistakes from
the batsman.

Swing Bowling

The prevailing atmospheric conditions will have a telling effect on the degree of swing of a ball.

For instance, a heavy atmosphere and good cloud cover are conducive to the ball swinging. If you are a swing bowler, remember the following to make the most of ideal conditions.

You should point the seam in the direction of the intended swing and polish only one side of the ball, making sure that there is no build up of dirt in the seam.

You can reduce the distance that the ball has to swing, by delivering as close to the stumps as possible.

Try to deliver the ball with your arm in as high a position as possible, this tends to make the ball swing late. This ball is more difficult for the batsman to play because he is likely to be committed to playing a shot in which the ball will move away from him.

Different degrees of swing can be achieved if you vary the pace of the delivery. A slight drop in pace for example, usually results in the ball swinging more.

The outswinger

The outswinger moves away in the air to the off-side when bowled to a right-handed batsman.

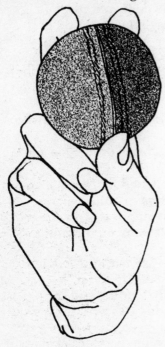

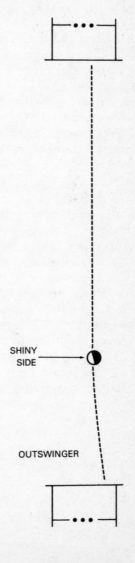

SHINY SIDE →

OUTSWINGER

Hold the ball with the seam vertical and pointing in the direction of first slip at the moment of delivery. Your first and second fingers are positioned either side of the seam and the right side of your thumb is at the bottom side of the ball, directly underneath them. The left side of your third finger is used to support the ball. The shiny side of the ball is pointing to the on-side.

In the action for the outswinger, your shoulder rotates more than normal. Move your left foot slightly more across to the on-side. Your back foot points in the direction of fine-leg. The ball is delivered from a high position and you keep your fingers in position behind the ball, for as long as possible. You should keep your wrist more rigid than usual. To generate the swing, a good body pivot is needed and a good follow-through. Swing your right arm down across your left thigh to complete the action.

The ball is pitched at the middle and off-stumps to make allowance for the swing. You may need to vary your grip, and position on the crease or line, as some balls swing more than others.

Ideally, the ball should be pitched at the batsman's pads as this requires little change in either grip or run-up. When bowled to a full length it is a very difficult ball to play, with the late swing moving the ball back towards the off-side.

If you move wider on the crease with the same amount of swing, you are more likely to hit the stumps. Alternatively, if you deliver the ball from close to the stumps and pitch it outside the leg-stump, you may bowl the batsman around his legs.

The outswinger is a useful ball to bowl to a batsman who favours hitting to the leg-side. It invariably induces him to hit across the line of the ball. If this is the case, maintain your line and length and set your field to encourage him to do this!

The inswinger

When the inswinger is pitched on or just outside off-stump, it moves in towards the batsman and away to the leg-side.

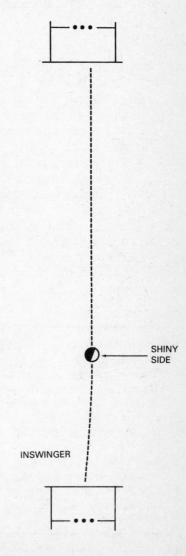

SHINY SIDE

INSWINGER

The grip is similar to that of the outswinger, but the shiny side of the ball is facing the off-side, with the seam of the ball still vertical and pointing towards fine leg. Your fingers are closer together on top of the seam than for the outswinger.

Once again there is a variation in the basic action for this ball.

Position your front foot further across to the off-side, with your eyes looking down the pitch from inside your front arm. Present more of your chest to the batsman prior to delivery and use your left side less. Deliver the ball from as high a position as possible, but unlike the delivery for the outswinger, your arm comes down the right side of your body instead of going across it. This helps to generate the swing towards leg.

The inswinger is a relatively easy ball to bowl but it demands a high degree of accuracy. If you are going to hit the wicket, you need to pitch the ball on or outside the off-stump.

The inswing bowler bowls from wider on the crease than the outswing bowler, to ensure the ball pitching on the off-side. A ball pitched on the stumps is going to pass aimlessly down the leg-side.

The aim with this ball is to try to keep the batsman playing off the front foot. You should keep the ball well up to him, and by varying the pace you may be able to bowl the batsman through bat and pad by hurrying him into his stroke.

LAW-BREAKER
You could have a run scored against you even if you bowl a no-ball, if the batsman hits it. He might be induced to hit it twice in which case he would be out, he can be run out on a no-ball too. In any event, the penalty of one run against your side will stand.

THE UMPIRE'S DECISION
NO BALL.

The off cutter
This ball is usually delivered by an outswing bowler
and it moves back off the pitch into the batsman.

Your first finger lies along the
seam, which is vertical and
pointing down the pitch at
the batsman. Your second
finger is placed close to it,
while your thumb is pressed
on to the seam underneath it.
As the ball is delivered, pull
your first finger down on the
seam, This imparts a
clockwise spin on the ball as
it is released, while your
hand rotates slightly, making
the ball come back at the
batsman.

The off cutter is a difficult ball to play when bowled
well, especially when the batsman is expecting the ball
to swing away from him. It can be disguised by using
the same follow-through as the outswinger.

The leg cutter

This is a ball mainly bowled by an in-swing bowler and when it is bowled well, it is another very difficult ball for the batsman to play. It should be pitched on middle or middle and off-stump and when pitched moves towards the off-side.

Like the inswinger, it is bowled from a high position and a good follow-through is important.

Hold the ball with the seam vertical and your second finger along the seam. Your first finger is placed alongside it, with your thumb pressed underneath on the seam.
When the ball is delivered, your second finger pulls down across the seam. By rotating your wrist, you add a slightly anti-clockwise spin on the ball, which when pitched leaves the batsman on the off-side.

Once again the leg cutter can be disguised easily, by following through as for an inswinger

Left Arm Seam Bowling

Left arm seam bowlers, whether fast or medium pace, should try to bowl from over the wicket. The ideal line of attack is to push the ball across the right-handed batsman, aiming mainly for a line about middle and off stumps. This induces the batsman to play inside the line of the ball, giving catches to the wicket-keeper or slips.

The natural swing of a left arm bowler is in to a right-handed bat. The batsman is usually preoccupied with the idea of the ball leaving him, so you may bowl him through the gap of bat and pad, to a ball that comes back at him.

You must liaise with your captain as to whether you are bowling the inswinger or a ball firing across the batsman, because of the difficulty of field placing.

LAW-BREAKER
If you bowl and the ball passes the batsman and yet is neither a wide nor a no-ball, provided it doesn't touch the batsman or his clothes the umpire may call a BYE, from which the batting side can score. Even if it does touch him, (though not his bat or batting hand) but in the opinion of the umpire was deflected, he can call a LEG-BYE.
Again if the batsman scores of this call his runs will stand.

THE UMPIRE'S DECISION
BYE, LEG-BYE He would have to judge whether the batsman tried to hit the ball with his bat or was trying to avoid being hit. It is possible that these two calls would be disallowed, if the ball has crossed the boundary for example. No penalty would be enforced in these circumstances.

Spin Bowling

There is no finer sight in cricket than the battle between a good spin bowler and a batsman.

With the advent of the one day game, the demand for spin bowlers seemed to wane as more and more captains looked upon spinners as a luxury. They turned instead to medium pace bowlers, to bowl line and length to keep down the runs.

Recently there has been a change of attitude with the realisation that spinners can in fact be match-winners.

One of the first points to make is that all aspiring spin bowlers should learn to spin the ball first, then develop line, length and flight and not the reverse. It is a skilful art with many variations.

You must also be able to adapt your bowling to different types of pitches. On good pitches, you will have to rely on flight, good length and direction. On others you will need to use a lower trajectory, push the ball through more quickly, maintain the necessary accuracy and still be able to make the ball turn.

LAW-BREAKER

In your efforts to unnerve the batsman, be careful not to bowl too high over or too wide of the wicket. If it is judged to be out of his reach, in his normal position the umpire will call 'WIDE'.

THE UMPIRE'S DECISION

You will have a run scored against you if he calls 'Wide'. It won't be a wide ball however if the batsman moves out of his normal 'guard' position, thus making the ball unreachable or moves into a position to hit it. If he scores from a wide, his runs will count.
You can still stump him.

The off spinner
In this ball the bowler imparts spin with his fingers, in a clockwise direction. The ball is delivered to move off the pitch from outside off-stump, in to the batsman.

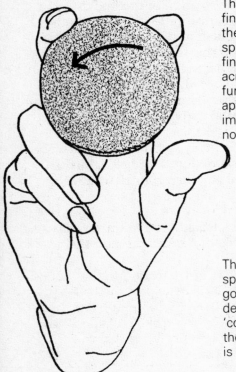

The top joint of your first finger grips the ball across the seam. This is the main spinning finger. Your second finger is widely spaced across the seam as well. The further these two fingers are apart the greater the spin imparted. Your thumb plays no part in this delivery at all.

The basic action of the off-spin bowler needs to be good. At the bottom of the delivery swing, your wrist is 'cocked' (wrist bent towards the thumb) so that your palm is facing upwards.

As the ball is delivered, the bowling arm is in as high a position as possible and your wrist is still cocked. At the point of release, ideally somewhere between one o'clock and eleven o'clock, your wrist flicks forward, with your first finger dragging sharply downwards in a clockwise direction. Your hand continues downwards after release, cutting across your body and finishes with the palm of your hand pointing upwards.

To obtain maximum bounce out of the pitch, use a short delivery stride and rise up on your toes using a high arm action and a straight front leg. One way to impart more spin is to get your front foot right across in front of the stumps and pivoting on it, drive the ball down the pitch using the rotation of the body.

The off-spinner must concentrate on spinning the ball, and deceiving the batsman. Flighting the ball is one of your major ploys. This is done by varying the actual release of the ball during the delivery. If the ball is released sooner than normal, it is given 'more air', ie. the ball is tossed higher than normal and may result in the batsman playing too early,.

If the ball is released later than normal, a flatter delivery is the result.

If the arm action is speeded up, the ball is pushed through a little more quickly than normal and may result in the batsman playing a hurried shot.

Variations in line may also add to the uncertainty of a batsman. Vary your position of delivery on the bowling crease.

You must be prepared to bowl around the wicket on a good turning pitch, to compensate for the ball turning so much, especially to a left-handed bat.

When the pitch is a slow-turner, the ball should be pushed through much more quickly, so that the batsman is rushed into his shots.

THE UMPIRE'S DECISION

The umpire's decision is final.

The bowling side can only appeal for a decision to call a batsman out if they do so before the bowler begins his delivery or run-up for the next ball. The appeal "HOW'S THAT?" covers all appeals to the umpire to declare a batsman out.

The floater
This is a ball used by an off-spinner and is a well disguised outswinger.

Viewed from down the wicket, the grip is the same as described for the off spin, but at the point of delivery the angle of the wrist is altered, so that the hand points down the wicket towards the batsman. The shiny side of the ball (if the bowler keeps the shine going) should be pointing towards the palm of the hand, spin is still imparted but unlike the off-spinner, it revolves around a vertical axis and drifts away to the off-side, hopefully deceiving the batsman.

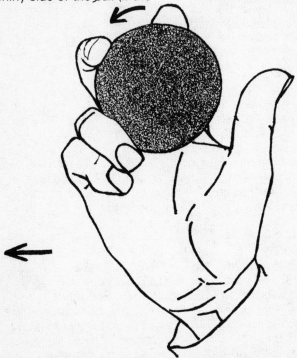

Keep the shine on one side of the ball as this helps when the ball is in flight, and all dirt should be cleaned from the seam to help the ball to bite on the pitch.

The leg spinner

The leg-break is a ball that is delivered to move off the pitch from the leg-side to the off-side of a right-handed batsman. This is achieved by the spin imparted by the fingers in an anti-clockwise direction.

Grip the ball with the top joint of your thumb and first two fingers. They should be naturally spaced apart and gripping across the seam. Your third finger cups the ball and lies along the seam to impart the leg spin. Your wrist is bent inwards towards your forearm and rotated outwards.

At the highest point of your delivery action, your wrist flips forward in the direction of the batsman. At the same time, your third and fourth fingers flick upwards and forwards and the thumb side of your hand cuts downwards, imparting the anti-clockwise spin.

Your right hand passes downwards and past your left thigh.

LAW-BREAKER
Remember to indicate to the umpire whether you intend to bowl over or under-arm, right or left-handed. Otherwise he will call a NO-BALL.
He will also call a no-ball if you throw rather than bowl the ball.

THE UMPIRE'S DECISION
No ball. Score one run, if none has been scored. He will define a ball as a "throw" if you straighten your arm immediately before the ball leaves your hand.

LAW-BREAKER
Be careful in your delivery stride. You must make sure your back foot doesn't land inside the return crease and that your front foot isn't behind the popping crease.

THE UMPIRE'S DECISION
No-ball Score one run, if none has been scored.

Unlike the off-spinner who can be used in a defensive role, the leg-spinner is usually used as an attacking bowler. His main line of attack should always be made over the wicket as it is essential for him to pitch accurately, as the difference between a good and bad ball is marginal.

You should keep the ball pitched well up to the batsman, inviting him to drive. Invariably, any ball pitched short, will result in him being hit to leg-side and is regarded a gift by most batsmen.

You should also bowl at the stumps, as you will not be able to gain an L.B.W. decision on any ball that is pitched outside leg-stump. A ball that is pitched up outside leg-stump will usually induce the sweep shot from a batsman and if not executed properly will result in the batsman top edging the ball into the air.

The only time that you should consider going round the wicket is to a left-hander. Then you should try to pitch the ball in the rough created by the bowler's follow-through, outside the left-hander's off-stump.

On fast, true pitches, concentrate on the off-stump of the right-hander and pack the off-side, especially the covers with fielders. This reduces the chances of getting the ball through and induces the batsman to hit across the line and against the spin, into the less populated on-side. Hopefully, he will then mis-hit the ball and be caught in the covers.

The googly

The grip for the googly is much like that of the leg-break but the action of the wrist differs in that it rotates sooner, so that the back of the wrist points towards the batsman and the palm away from him. The finger movement works in the same way as for the leg-break.

However, because your hand is rotated, the ball leaves your hand, over the third and fourth fingers and the spin imparted is the same as for the off-spin. This means that the ball will pitch and move away to the leg-side.

Because the movement of the wrist needs more rotation, your front foot moves slightly to the off-side which tends to open your chest. Your left shoulder drops and your bowling arm swings higher. In the follow-through, your bowling arm finishes pointing down the wicket, with the palm of the hand facing out towards square-leg.

The googly should be used as a surprise ball and should be bowled so that the batsman still thinks that he is batting to a leg-break and the ball hits the stumps.

To do this, the ball should be pitched on the off-stump or just outside, so that the spin does not take the ball wide of leg-stump.

When the bowler has been attacking the off-stump consistently and then pitches the ball well wide of off-stump, the batsman would quickly sense that the googly is being bowled and would not play it as a leg-break.

You should lead up to the occasional googly, by bowling a succession of leg-breaks more to the off-side, before sending the googly down at the batsman. If the batsman is known for playing the googly, avoid bowling it. He will then think that one is going to be bowled. In this way he may be indecisive and offer a catch to the keeper or slips.

The top spinner

The grip used for the top spinner is the same as that of the leg-break. The main difference is that for the top spinner, the wrist rotates sooner than in the leg-break. The spin is thus imparted down the line of the flight, picking up pace and not deviating towards the slips but going straight on. It is very hard to control this ball so that after pitching it does not move to leg or off-side.

The top spinner is best used on a fast pitch to a back foot batsman. If he misjudges the length of the delivery, he may be beaten by the quicker pace off the wicket, resulting in a wicket for the bowler.

Left arm spin bowling

A left arm spin bowler usually moves the ball from leg to off-side of the right- handed batsman and as such uses the same grip as the off-spin bowler.

You should concentrate on variation of pace and flight and bowling round the wicket at the off-stump. If faced by a left-handed batsman, convert your attack to over the wicket and concentrate on pitching the ball in the bowler's rough outside the batsman's off-stump.

When bowling on a turning wicket, keep the ball well up to the batsman and induce the drive. If the ball is turning quite appreciably, then move slip and gulley wider than usual.

One of the most successful left arm spin deliveries is the 'Chinaman'. This is an off-break bowled by the left-armer to a right-handed batsman. It is successful because it is rare for batsmen to play to this type of bowling and therefore it creates indecision.

Field Placings for Different Types of Bowling

Different types of bowling require a wide variety of fielding positions, too numerous to describe. The following placings outline the basic, orthodox fielding positions usually employed by most captains and bowlers.

There are bound to be adjustments to these placings, depending on the position of the game, the type of batsman, change in atmospheric conditions, the state of the pitch etc.

Once the captain and bowler have set a field and decided on the tactics to be employed, it is up to the bowler to bowl to this. Your captain can't compensate for his bowler's shortcomings. If you stray from line

THE UMPIRE'S DECISION
The umpire will call a dead ball in a great variety of circumstances. For example, when:-
the wicket-keeper or bowler has finally caught it safely in his hands; it has gone over the boundary; the batsman is out;
it has got caught up in the batsman's clothes or indeed the umpire's, or one of your own fielding side's and when a penalty score has already been awarded.

The ball will also be dead at the end of an over; after an injury; when play is unfair; when the batsman doesn't try to play the shot because he isn't ready or the bowler fails to bowl. Finally if the bails fall off before the ball is delivered or the umpire has to move, he will call no ball.

LAW-BREAKER
If you fail to pick-up the ball before it reaches the boundary you will usually have 4 runs scored against your side. If the ball actually goes well over the boundary it will be 6 runs. You must also be careful to keep your balance. You can have a 6 scored against you, if you take the ball over the boundary; even if you caught it cleanly.

THE UMPIRE'S DECISION
He won't give a 6 if the ball hits the sight screen when it is within the playing area. If the umpire at the bowler's end signals a boundary it will be because the ball touched the boundary, or you do so with the ball in your hand. Obviously if the batsman has made runs before the boundary is called and they number more than 4 or 6 they will count.

and length the batsman will gain the advantage and this will have an adverse effect on your colleagues' confidence.

So it is essential that you concentrate all the time and try to spot flaws in the batsman's defence and react accordingly.

LAW-BREAKER
Don't lose your temper out of frustration and throw the ball wilfully over the boundary or both the boundary and any runs made will be scored against you.

Fielding positions to a right-hand batsman

The boundary of the playing area is agreed by the umpires and captains before the toss, and is marked, if possible in full with a white line, rope on the ground or fence. If it is only possible to use intermittent flags or markers then an imaginary line between them defines the boundary.

Sight-screens inside, or partly inside, the playing area count as part of the boundary if the ball hits or goes over or under them.

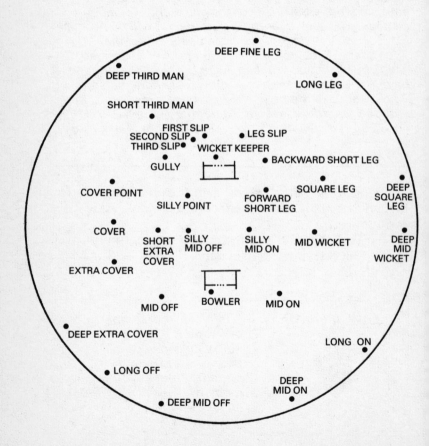

DEEP FINE LEG

DEEP THIRD MAN

LONG LEG

SHORT THIRD MAN

FIRST SLIP
SECOND SLIP
THIRD SLIP
WICKET KEEPER
LEG SLIP

GULLY
BACKWARD SHORT LEG

COVER POINT
SQUARE LEG
DEEP SQUARE LEG

SILLY POINT
FORWARD SHORT LEG

COVER

SHORT EXTRA COVER
SILLY MID OFF
SILLY MID ON
MID WICKET
DEEP MID WICKET

EXTRA COVER

MID OFF
BOWLER
MID ON

DEEP EXTRA COVER

LONG ON

LONG OFF
DEEP MID ON

DEEP MID OFF

Defensive medium pace bowling

When there is little swing or movement off the wicket, the bowler must concentrate on bowling defensively, ie. keeping down the runs and frustrating the batsman into mistakes. Your line of attack should be on or just outside off-stump and packing the off-side field, attempt to induce the batsman to hit to the leg-side.

In this formation gully (A) has moved to point , an extra-cover fielder brought in and long-leg brought up to mid-wicket for the mis-timed shot.

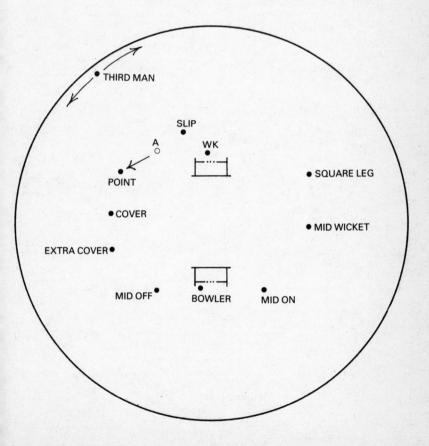

Fast/medium, inswing

This is regarded as the orthodox field for the medium pace inswing bowler.

Five fielders are on the off-side and four on the on-side, although some bowlers may prefer to have an extra man on the on-side usually moving gully across to mid-wicket position (A). When the ball is not swinging too much, square leg will move backwards to cut off any singles. Long leg and third man, as in the case of the outswinger, can be positioned wider or finer as the situation dictates.

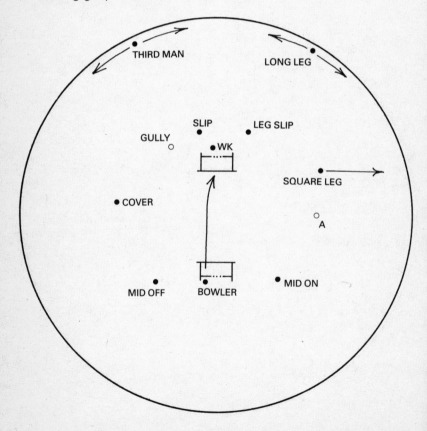

THIRD MAN

LONG LEG

SLIP

LEG SLIP

GULLY

WK

SQUARE LEG

COVER

A

MID OFF

BOWLER

MID ON

Fast/medium, outswing

The orthodox field for the medium pace outswing bowler is the 6/3 field. Six men are positioned on the off-side and three on the leg-side. When the ball is swinging considerably, square-leg will move across to third slip position (A) while mid-on will move wider to the mid-wicket position (B) to cut off any singles on the leg-side. Long-leg and third man can be positioned finer or wider according to how much the ball is swinging.

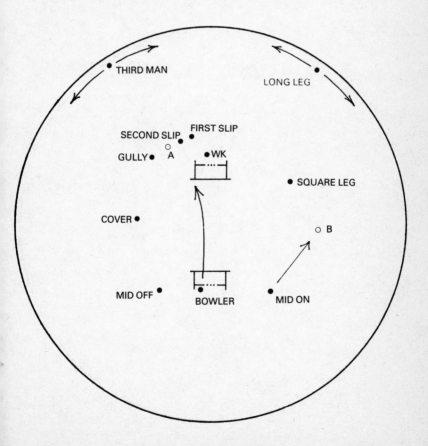

Off spin

With the field set for the orthodox spin bowler on a true pitch, concentrate your line of attack over the wicket to just outside off-stump. The batsman is forced to take risks when attempting to avoid hitting the ball into the area covered by the fielders. If the batsman succeeds in getting through the off-side, the bowler should strengthen this area by bringing deep mid-wicket across to extra cover (A) and moving cover squarer.

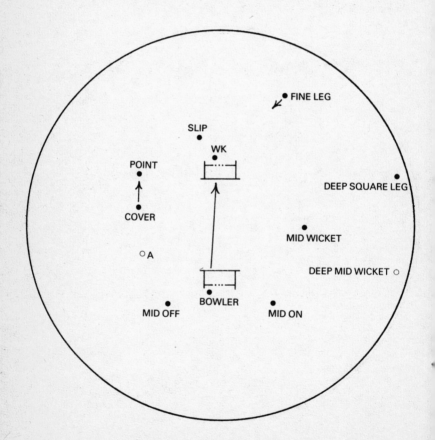

Turning pitch

When the ball is turning quite appreciably, attack the batsman from around the wicket, keeping the ball up to the batsman, to make him play consistently on the front foot. If the batsman is having difficulty against this line of attack, you could dispense with your slip and make another forward short-leg (A), move point to short third man (B) bringing mid-wicket straighter and moving mid-on to deep mid-wicket (C). When bowling to this field, accuracy is of vital importance, so that the fielders in the close catching positions, avoid injury.

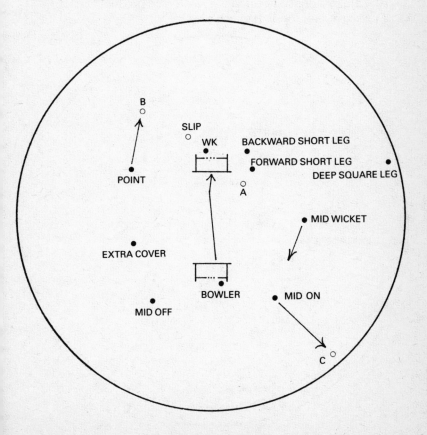

Leg spin/googly

By bowling over the wicket and attacking the batsman's off-stump the leg spin bowler should try to force the batsman into playing the ball into the off-side. If using this tactic, pack the off-side to tempt the batsman to hit across the line to the leg-side and against the spin, resulting in a possible catch in the covers. If the batsman hits over the top of the fielders then deep extra-cover can be moved deeper, to position (B) as shown in the diagram. If the batsman successfully hits to leg, then deep extra cover can be moved over to mid-wicket (A) and mid-on moves to deep mid-wicket (C) in an effort to produce a catch.

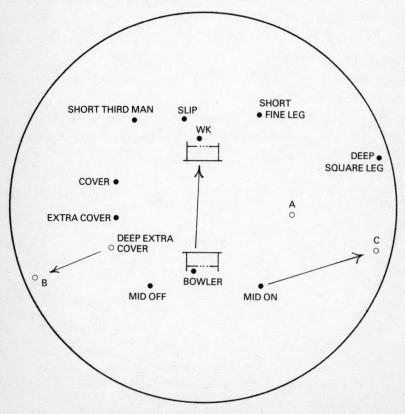

Turning pitch

On a turning pitch, the bowler should bowl over the wicket and in the direction of off-stump. Accuracy is of paramount importance. If bowling along this line, you should have two slips to improve the chances of getting a catch. If the batsman is defensive, you could move extra cover up to silly mid-off (A) and keep the batsman on the front foot. If he tries to hit across the line and pulls the ball against the spin, deep square- leg may be moved wider into a deeper mid-wicket position (B) for a possible catch.

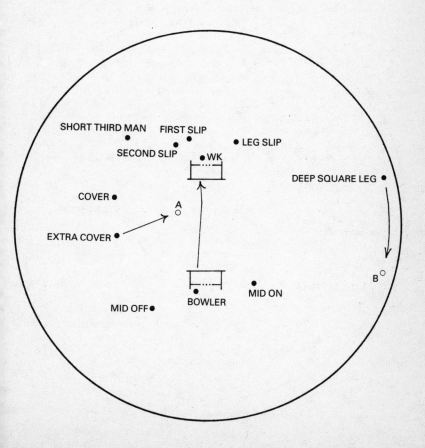

Slow left arm

The slow left arm bowler should attack from around the wicket and on or just outside off-stump, keeping the ball well up to the batsman in an effort to get him to drive the ball. Most of the fielders are in deep catching positions on the off-side, but extra cover may be moved up to a much shorter position in case the batsman mis-times the drive to give a simple catch.

The leg-side field may be moved around depending on the batsman, e.g. mid-on moving deeper, mid-wicket round to mid-on and short fine-leg round to deep mid-wicket.

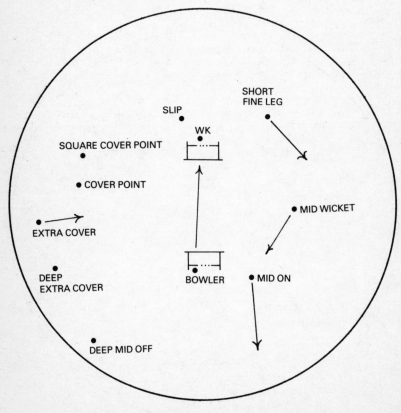

SHORT FINE LEG

SLIP

WK

SQUARE COVER POINT

COVER POINT

EXTRA COVER

MID WICKET

DEEP
EXTRA COVER

BOWLER

MID ON

DEEP MID OFF

Turning pitch

On a turning pitch, the slow left arm bowler should concentrate his attack around the wicket, pitching the ball well up to the batsman on middle-stump. The ball may not need as much spin but will need greater accuracy. If the ball is turning more than usual, first slip should move wider and second slip should move into the gulley position. For an attacking batsman, move silly mid-off back into the covers, position (C). The leg-side field positions can also be adjusted for different batsmen.

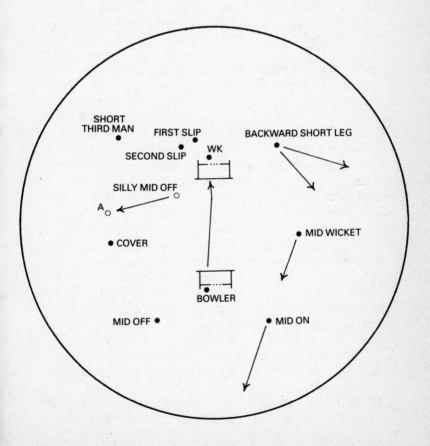

Fielding

Fielding plays a very important part in cricket and every player can improve this aspect of his game. Any batsman will find it difficult to score against an alert and well organised fielding side. The pressure exerted on him by good fielding can have a vital bearing on the result of a match, as he can be forced into errors. For while it is the object of the batting side to score as many runs as possible, it still remains the aim of the fielding side to bowl out the opposition, for as few runs as possible.

One of the oldest clichés in cricket is 'Catches win Matches', and how many times in the course of a match has this been proved so? A vital catch 'put down' can be the turning point and while it is not always possible, you should try to hold on to every catch. Confidence plays a great part in this. If there is any doubt in your mind about the success of a catch, you will probably drop it. Think positive at all times!

The fielding abilities of every player will be taken into account before arriving at a final team selection. There is nothing more disheartening for a bowler than to give his all, when the fielders are lethargic and disinterested. The batsman will soon get on top and lack of interest from the fielders gives him confidence to play his shots.

The selection of captain is also very important. Not only should he be a key member of the team at either batting or bowling, he should also be a good fielder, so that he can lead by example and generate a good team spirit.

Team spirit is one of the keys to good fielding, encouragement rather than criticism can mean a great deal to a player who has dropped a catch or mis-fielded the ball.

So what are the qualities that make a good fielder?

The main qualities are physical fitness, mental alertness and concentration.

LAW-BREAKER
If the ball in play is lost beyond recall, any fielder can call "LOST BALL". If the batsman has hit the ball, he will automatically score 6 runs, unless of course he has already run more than 6, in which case the runs made will be taken as his score, including any he is taking at the moment when lost ball is called. He will have to have crossed with the other batsman before the call goes up.
If he hadn't hit the ball before it was lost then the score of byes, no-balls, etc will be registered.

Fitness, Mental Alertness and Concentration

It reflects very badly on the team if a fielding side
includes players who are unfit. In fact an unfit player
can be a fielding sides' biggest liability. So it is
essential that you try to become as fit as possible.

Mental alertness and the ability to concentrate are of
great importance. A good fielder should be thinking
about the game constantly, watching the batsman and
looking for any faults in technique that may result in
the bad shots that produce wickets. You should keep
a constant eye on the captain, particularly during the
course of an over, for any field-placing changes.

Study your own bowlers too, to improve your
knowledge, effectiveness and anticipation of where the
ball is going to be hit.

All fielders, apart from those in close catching
positions, should 'walk in' towards the batsman as the
bowler runs up, so that they can move quickly on to
the path of the ball, the moment it has been struck.

You should always back one another up in the field.
There are many ways in which this can be done.

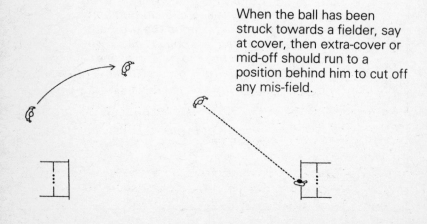

When the ball has been
struck towards a fielder, say
at cover, then extra-cover or
mid-off should run to a
position behind him to cut off
any mis-field.

Equally, if a ball has been struck through the in-field towards the boundary and there is no deep fielder, the two fielders bisected by the ball should chase it to the boundary. This way, if one stops the ball just inside the boundary line and his speed takes his body over the boundary by a few yards, the other can by slowing down his speed a split second earlier, pick the ball up and return it to the wicket-keeper.

Once the ball is returned to the wicket, it is the responsibility of the fielders behind both the wicket-keeper and the fielder covering the stumps at the non-striker's end, to position themselves in line with the thrower, in case of any mis-field.

Concentration is most important to fielding, and the captain can help a player's power of concentration during the course of any innings. He should try to keep his players in the game at all times. Long spells of inactivity on the boundary, especially in hot, sunny weather are the easiest ways for a fielder to lose his concentration. A good captain will try to move all his players about, apart from his specialist fielders, to generate interest when it is waning.

Calling

Another important aspect of good fielding is 'calling'.
How many times have two players gone for the same
catch? They either run into each other, or leave it to
one another and the ball falls harmlessly between
them. It is really the responsibility of the player nearest
the ball to call 'mine'. If neither player calls, the
captain or another fielder needs to intervene and name
one of the players attempting the catch. The one called
should then concentrate on the ball, while the other
stops running so as not to put him off.

Practice, above all else is the key to good fielding
there are various ways to practise all aspects of
fielding.

Ground Fielding

The speed of the ball, its direction and the distance
from the wicket, determine the technique to be used
for intercepting.

When a quick pick-up and return is needed, use the
attacking interception. There are two most often used
methods of attacking interceptions: underarm, when
close to the wicket, or overarm, when further away.

Accuracy is vital when throwing from these
positions.

The long barrier

The 'long barrier' is generally referred to as the defensive interception and is used to field a fast moving ball in the out-field. Usually there is only 'one run' and a clean, safe stop and quick return are the main objectives.

Although this is termed defensive, a good throw from the long barrier position can run out the batsman trying for a quick second run.

Once you have determined the line of the ball, take up position, by bending down with your left knee directly behind your right heel (right-handed throwers), square to the line of the ball. Your hands should be spread in front of your left knee, with fingers pointing downwards to the ground. This forms a barrier to prevent the ball passing. Your head is over your left knee, eyes level with the ground, watching the ball into your hands.

Always wait for the ball to reach your hands (never snatch). When the pick-up is complete, push up with your weight on your right foot and turn your shoulders. Point your left arm, fully stretched in the direction of the target. Your throwing arm comes through with your weight transferring to your left foot, as your body pivots with the impetus of the throw. Finish with your throwing arm in the direction of the target and your left arm thrown back behind your left shoulder. Your eyes should be still fixed on the target.

Attacking interception

The attacking interception is used by a fielder moving quickly on to a ball.

You should attack on the line of the ball, moving in quickly and stamp your right foot down firmly on the ground, at right-angles to the line of the ball.

Get down, with your hands in front of your right foot, fingers pointing down. Your head will be over your right foot, eyes fixed firmly on the ball, watching it into your hands. As you complete the pick-up, your right hand draws back and upwards behind your right shoulder, while you push your body up on your right foot. Bring your left arm up, to point fully outstretched, in the direction of the target. Your trailing left leg is brought through to move into the throwing position. The throw is completed as for the long barrier.

Close to the wicket interception (underarm throw)

This interception is used when fielding close to the wicket and there is a possibility of a run-out with the batsmen going for a quick single.

Approach the ball at speed with your head down and eyes fixed firmly on the ball. The balance of your body will be forward and your throwing arm poised, hanging downwards to receive the ball. Pick up the ball at the side of your foot, which is parallel to the line of the ball, and in the same movement draw it backwards.

Continue the run and as your left foot comes through, followed by the right, throw the ball underarm, at the target. Keep your head still throughout, with eyes fixed firmly on the ball until you have picked it up, then transfer to the target.

Interception Practice.

There are various ways of practising to improve intercepting a ball and returning it to the wicket.

The long barrier
This can be practised almost anywhere on a flat surface.

1. Two fielders stand opposite one another, approximately 50 yards apart. The first fielder rolls the ball underarm at speed towards his partner, who should then intercept the ball as described. He should concentrate on the push up into the throwing position and return the ball to his partner with an accurate throw.

Repeat 6 times, then swap over and repeat the sequence.

2. For a full scale practice, set up the stumps.
The wicket-keeper stands up and behind the stumps. The fielders line up, approximately 50 yards away from the stumps and the coach or nominated person throws the ball at speed, along the ground to the first man in the line. He intercepts it, using the correct method and returns it to the wicket-keeper.

The sequence is repeated along the line.

This practice both improves the pick-up and allows the player to judge the ideal length of the throw into the wicket-keeper's hands, at about stump-height.

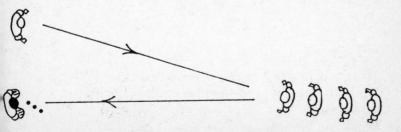

Attacking interception (overarm)

It is most important to practise the pick-up when using the attacking interception, as speed is of the essence.

1. This can be done quite easily by placing a tennis ball on the ground. The fielder then 'retires' to a distance about 10 yards away. He 'attacks' the ball at speed as described. He picks the ball up and pushes up into the throwing position, with his left arm pointing in the direction of an imaginary target.

Do this as many times as it takes to master the technique.

2. For group practice, use the same layout as for the long barrier interception. The difference is that in this case, the fielder attacks the ball at speed. This practice demonstrates the importance of pointing the non-throwing arm at the target or the throw will not be accurate.

Attacking interception (underarm throw)

For the most effective practice, set up some stumps with a line of fielders about 20 yards away. From behind the stumps, the server rolls the ball out at speed along the ground, towards the line of fielders. The first fielder attacks the ball and using the correct pick-up returns the ball underarm, at the stumps.

The sequence is repeated along the line of fielders in turn.

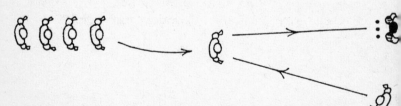

Regular practice of this exercise for close fielders, will both improve and maintain accuracy and alertness.

Retrieving

One of the most important skills in fielding is retrieving the ball when it has been struck past the fielder.

There are two basic techniques to study: one for the slow moving or stationary ball and one for the faster moving ball.

The slow moving ball

The slow moving or stationary ball is picked up against the left foot. When making a long throw it is important to get a strong push, back against your left foot, to add the momentum to make the throw, without the need to run into the throwing position.

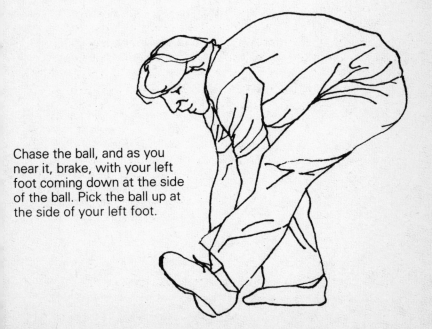

Chase the ball, and as you near it, brake, with your left foot coming down at the side of the ball. Pick the ball up at the side of your left foot.

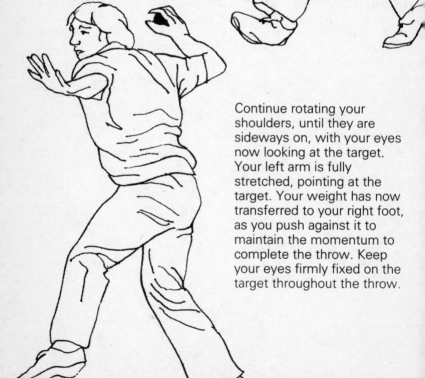

Now the push on your left foot begins. As the push up continues, straighten your left leg as your right foot moves into a square position. Start to rotate your shoulders, with your front arm turning to face the target and your right arm coming up into the throwing position.

Continue rotating your shoulders, until they are sideways on, with your eyes now looking at the target. Your left arm is fully stretched, pointing at the target. Your weight has now transferred to your right foot, as you push against it to maintain the momentum to complete the throw. Keep your eyes firmly fixed on the target throughout the throw.

The fast moving ball

The pick-up of the fast moving ball differs from that of the slow moving ball, in that it is picked up at the side of your right foot.

Chase the ball and move alongside it. Bend quickly, with your eyes fixed on the ball. Stamp your right foot down firmly on the ground, with the outside of your foot at the side of the ball. Pick up the ball from this position and push off on your right foot, turning your shoulders, so your left shoulder points towards the target. Draw your right arm upwards and backwards, level with your shoulders and point your left arm, outstretched at the target. Turn your head until your eyes are looking at the target. Keep them fixed on the target until the throw has been completed.

Throwing on the turn
This throw is usually used when retrieving a ball close to the wicket. The approach is the same as that for the fast moving ball.

Pick the ball up against the outside of your right foot. Point your left arm quickly back towards the target, as the rapid turn and pivot on your left foot begins. (The jump-off on your left foot allows you to make a throw of limited length). This takes

you up into the throwing
position. Throw the ball
quickly and as the follow-
through is completed, land
with your weight on your
right foot and your eyes still
on the target.

Retrieving Practice

As with intercepting, there are various ways of practising retrieving.

Once again speed and accuracy are at the heart of good retrieval. Practice for improving speed and pick-up technique can be done with the following exercises.

The first exercise can be carried out on any flat area, (tarmac or grass).

1. Using groups of 4 or 5, position groups in a line behind skittles. Using tennis balls or indoor plastic balls, the coach starts a relay race. The second man in the line, rolls the ball out underarm in the direction shown. The first man, on the word "go", retrieves the ball at speed and using correct pick-up technique, returns the ball to the line, where number 3 catches it. He rolls it out underarm for number 2, who returns the ball to number 4, who rolls to number 3.

The sequence is continued until 2 complete turns have been made and number 1 has returned to the front of the line. This can be repeated as many times as it takes to improve technique and speed.

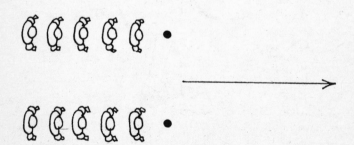

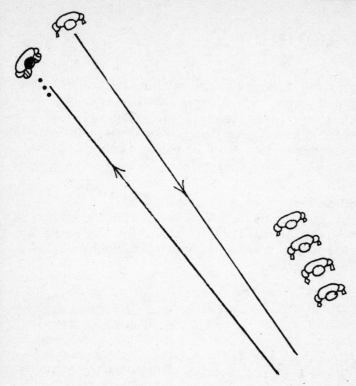

2. Set up a set of stumps. The coach throws the ball out past a line of fielders. The first man retrieves the ball and returns it to the wicket-keeper, who is standing behind the stumps in line with the ball. This exercise should improve the accuracy of the fielder's throwing.

These are just a couple of exercises to improve technique and accuracy but variations can be used. Practice needs to be enjoyable as well as being taken seriously, so try to vary routines, so that they do not become boring and mundane.

Remember too, fielders should always expect the ball to come to them and should always watch the ball into their hands.

Catching

'Catches win Matches', and catching falls basically into two categories: high catching and close catching.

There are three golden rules to follow to be successful at catching; Watch the ball into your hands, let your hands give with the ball and keep your head still unless it is a running catch.

High catching

When you are taking a catch away from the wicket, first judge the flight of the ball and then move quickly on to the line. It is always easier to move forwards than backwards.

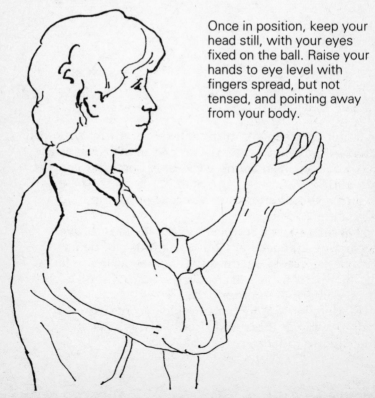

Once in position, keep your head still, with your eyes fixed on the ball. Raise your hands to eye level with fingers spread, but not tensed, and pointing away from your body.

Watch the ball into your hands which should close round the ball at contact, at the same time 'giving' with your hands, to finish with the ball close to your chest.

It is most important to 'give' with the ball as this absorbs the shock of it, as it makes contact with your hands and helps the closing of your hands round the ball.

An alternative method when the ball is dropping out of the sun, is to hold your hands above the level of your eyes, with the palms of your hands pointing away from your body towards the ball.

Spread your fingers, pointing upwards with thumbs crossed and locked together. Keep your head still, with your eyes looking through spread fingers. This helps to break up the glare of the sun. As the ball makes contact with your hands, let them give.

Your hands and the ball come to rest over your right or left shoulder.

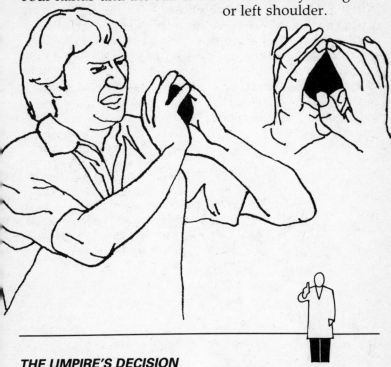

THE UMPIRE'S DECISION

He will decide that a catch is fair if you were within the field of play for the entire process of making the catch. The beginning of that process will start as soon as you touch the ball and will be concluded as soon as you have the ball fully under control, unless you go out of the field of play in the process. You mustn't touch the ground with the ball or catch the ball on your helmet. If it lodges in your clothes by accident it will still be a fair catch however.

You can also claim the catch if the batsman struck it twice, as long as it hasn't touched the ground in between and if it the ball bounces off an obstruction unless it has already been agreed that the obstacle forms part of the boundary.

Close catching

When fielding close to the wicket, you should concentrate hard on every delivery. In general, all close fielders, excluding the wicket-keeper and first slip, should keep their eyes firmly fixed on the bat.

On taking up position, keep down low with your knees and hips bent. The weight of your body is evenly distributed on the balls of your feet, which are relaxed. The palms of your hands face the batsman, with fingers pointing down. Keep your head still and slightly forward of your knees and your eyes level with the ground. Your elbows should be away from your legs and not resting on them, as this restricts free arm movement.

FAULT-FINDER

It is essential that you stay down until the shot has been completed and that you do not anticipate the stroke. As in high catching, you should watch the ball into your hands, which should give with the ball.

Skim catch

This catch is used when the ball is travelling towards you at head-height.

Your hands make a 'trap' for the ball, with thumbs pointing upwards. Aim to catch the ball in front of your face. Move your head out of the line of the ball just before the ball makes contact with your hands. Your hands should give with the ball, to finish just above your right or left shoulder.

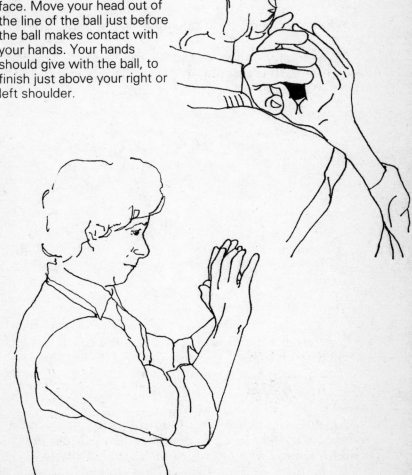

Practice

Practice at catching gives the confidence that can only come with the ability to catch the ball consistently.

When practising high catching, don't be content to stand still and let the ball be thrown or hit to you. The coach should vary the distance and direction so that you have to judge the flight and take catches on the run or moving backwards.

When practising close catching the methods can vary.

1. For small groups the 'cradle' can be used. This is where the ball is thrown on the cradle and because of its shape, comes off at different angles.

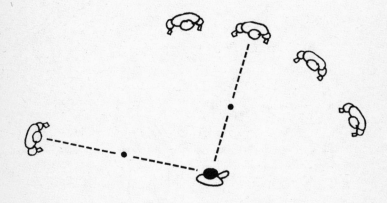

2. Alternatively for group practice, the coach can hit a ball thrown to him, towards the fielders who are spaced about 3 yards apart in an arc, about 8 – 10 yards away from the bat.

3. Another practice is for the fielders to form a circle of approximately 10 yards diameter. They throw the ball underarm, at random, to each other. This also helps to improve the reflexes of the close fielder.

Wicket-keeping

The wicket-keeper is one of the most important members of any cricket side. If this is your role, your first responsibility is to help the bowlers to dismiss batsmen. You need to be always alert and concentrate fully for the whole of the innings. You can inspire your team with good takes, or give words of encouragement to flagging team mates.

The captain relies on the wicket-keeper because he is always in the action. You should be able to pick up weaknesses in the batsmen's technique and relay this information to the captain, who can then rearrange his field or line of attack to play on these weaknesses.

You must try always to catch every ball, from whatever angle or wherever it pitches. When the fielder makes a good throw from the deep, straight into the gloves, acknowledge this, it inspires the fielder.

Set your sights to maximise the chances of dismissals, and minimise the errors, as it is this ability that separates a top class wicket-keeper from an average one.

There are three main factors to successful wicket-keeping: Good balance, good footwork and good technique and two basic positions : Standing up, and standing back.

Wicket-keepers should stand right up to the wicket or right back, never half-way.

The Stance

The stance should be as comfortable as possible, as you will have to go into the position many times during the course of an innings.

Your body should be right down, with your knees fully bent and feet suitably positioned, to give a good view of every delivery. Stand with them comfortably apart, with heels raised off the ground, for maximum mobility. Hold your hands together, with fingers pointing down and palms facing the bowler. Keep your head still, eyes level with the ground and firmly fixed on the ball.

Taking the ball-standing back

When taking the ball standing back, take up the stance position, slightly forward and two full arms-lengths from first-slip.

As the ball pitches, rise with the ball into a crouching position. Bring your hands together slightly forward of your body, to allow them to give as the ball is taken. Your palms should still be facing the ball, with fingers pointing downwards. Distribute your weight evenly on both feet, to enable quick movement to either side. Fix your eyes firmly on the ball and level with the ground. Ideally, the ball should be taken on the downward trajectory, in as comfortable a position as possible, between knee and waist-height. Keep your eyes level and move your weight on to the line of the ball.

FAULT-FINDER
It is important that the ball is taken in the area between knee and waist as one of the common faults of wicket-keepers is to stand too far back, or too close.

Taking a rising ball – close to the wicket
When taking the ball standing close to the wicket, keep within an imaginary semi-circle, approximately one full stride radius from the centre stump.

From the 'stance' position, rise with the ball, keeping your eyes firmly fixed on it. Your head and body should be directly behind the line of the ball, with your elbows free from your sides. Keep your palms facing the ball, with fingers pointing down. The ball is taken close to the wicket and directly below the eyes. Your weight should be on the foot nearest to the stumps, to allow greater hand movement towards the stumps.

Taking on the off-side – standing up

When taking a wider ball on the off-side while standing up, start by crouching down in the 'stance' position, with your weight evenly distributed on each foot.

As the ball pitches, rise with it, keeping your body poised forwards and towards the stumps, until you pick up the line of the ball. Move your outside foot out but not back, getting your body on to the line of the ball. The weight of your body is now on the outside foot which should be turned in towards the stumps. Keep your head down. The palms of your hands should still be facing the ball, with fingers pointing down. As the ball makes contact with your gloves, let your hands give with the ball and at the same time transfer your weight rapidly, from the outside to the inside foot. This gives you the momentum to bring your hands through to the stumps for a possible stumping.

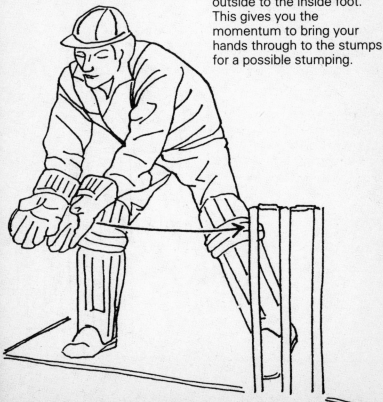

Taking the wider ball—standing up on leg-side

When you are taking the ball on the leg-side, do not move too quickly. Stay crouched down in the 'stance' position with your weight evenly distributed on each foot, until the ball has pitched and you have picked up the exact line. Once you have picked up the line, you must move quickly into position on the leg-side.

Transfer your weight on to your inside foot (left foot) and at the same time, cross your outside foot (right foot), behind your inside leg.

This transfers your weight to your right foot, which has come to rest with toes turned in towards the stumps. Bring your left foot across, in front of your right leg, on to the line of the ball.
Your toes are pointing in towards the stumps.

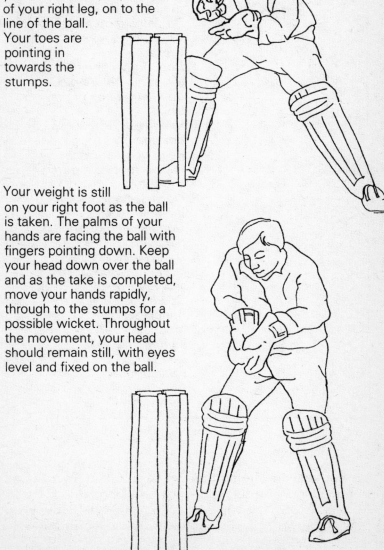
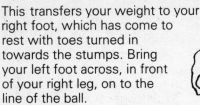

Your weight is still on your right foot as the ball is taken. The palms of your hands are facing the ball with fingers pointing down. Keep your head down over the ball and as the take is completed, move your hands rapidly, through to the stumps for a possible wicket. Throughout the movement, your head should remain still, with eyes level and fixed on the ball.

FAULT-FINDER

1. Do you stand in 'no-man's land'?
2. Do you keep your eye on the ball at all times?.
3. Do you get up too early when standing up to the wicket?
4. Don't move to either side too early, before picking up the true line of the ball.
5. Keep your head as still as possible.
6. Keep good balance.
7. Is your footwork good enough?
8. Do your fingers rather than palms face the ball?
9. Don't snatch or grab at the ball.
10. Don't hesitate when going for wide balls, once decided – go all the way.
11. Do you use the pads unnecessarily?
12. Maintain your equipment well!
13. Don't lose concentration.

Wicket-keepers should practise hard, taking every type of bowling. By studying the bowler's hand and body actions closely you will be able to read each delivery bowled by your bowlers in the course of an innings.

You need to practise in the nets, with or without batsmen present, especially where a specific technique needs improvement. You should only use the nets when there is enough room behind the stumps and then only to bowlers to whom you would normally stand up.

When fielding back from the stumps, you must run up to the wicket as quickly as possible for return throws and when in position, raise an arm as a guide to the thrower.

Always try to return the ball at a catchable height, when you return it to a fielder or bowler.

As you become more experienced, you should attempt to 'take' the ball to the wicket with your strongest hand. Whether the ball is taken on the off-side or leg-side of the wicket, using the 'one-handed' technique can greatly enhance the speed of the action of taking the ball to the stumps for a possible stumping.

Finally, you must always wear the correct equipment, that is pads, gloves, box and in sunny weather, a hat.

The Captain

The role of the captain
The captain of a cricket team is probably the most prestigious position in the club. It is his responsibility both to captain the team, and to carry out the policies of those who elected him, both on and off the field of play.

If you are the captain, then you are arguably the most influential captain of any team in sport. This should be some compensation for the fact that your responsibilities are awesome! Depending on your actions, you can dictate the course of a game to the enjoyment, or displeasure, not only of the players but also the spectators.

A positive approach to win every match from the first delivery must be your first aim, this will make the game interesting and enjoyable. If however, during the course of the game you feel that a victory is not possible, your next objective is to ensure that your team does not lose. How you do this can have a significant effect on your players' confidence.

You need to gain the respect of all your players. You may not always be the most skilled player in the side, but you can go a long way to achieving this, by unselfish performance and 100% application. You will have to believe in firm discipline and good sportsmanship. For instance, if the need arises to admonish a player, this should be done in private. You will lose their respect, and rightly so if you ridicule players on the field.

A good captain should have a good knowledge of the rules and be well versed in the game. You will need to study tactics and put them to good use. You will also have to know the capabilities of all the players in your squad, their strengths and weaknesses and allow for these in your decisions.

A cricket team is not just made up of players, you should appreciate and acknowledge the efforts of people working behind the scenes, and don't forget there are many. Etiquette demands that you are always polite, especially when welcoming the opposing side.

You will also have to make sure that no matter how hard-fought the game, it is always played in a sporting manner and make your side understand that the umpire's decision is final and not to show dissent on the field of play.

What are the rewards of this position? Well, the captain should always be a member of the 'selection committee' and ought to have a major influence on the selection of the team, but remember, it is not your right to pick the team.

When the final team has been selected, it is your not always pleasant duty to inform players not selected about their exclusion in an honest and sincere way. You will need to explain the reasons why they have not been selected, offering words of encouragement and advice.

Always discuss the tactics before the start of the game and listen to any comments and ideas from your players. A good captain will always listen to his men and assess their comments and not dismiss them lightly. Good Luck!

Winning The Toss

The team which wins the toss can choose whether to bat or field and many factors influence this decision. Before going out to 'toss', the captain will glean as much information as possible on the atmospheric conditions prevailing; the forecast over the duration of the match; the state of the pitch; the strength of the opposition and the type of match being played.

If the pitch is firm and no rain is forecast, then a captain will usually decide to bat first. This is because at the start of the match the pitch is usually at its best, but will deteriorate as the game goes on, causing the bounce to become unpredictable. This may not be significant during one-day or afternoon matches, where if the pitch has been well prepared, the wear will be minimal.

If the pitch is damp, then the surface may not withstand the impact of the ball, resulting in pieces being taken out and making the bounce unpredictable. In this case batting second is usually the choice.

If the pitch is wet, then it becomes very difficult for the bowlers to grip the ball firmly. The bowlers will lose accuracy and be unable to swing or spin the ball. In this situation, though the outfield may be slow, the batsman will always have the advantage, so the decision should be to bat.

If the pitch is hard and the grass has not been cut short, this will allow the ball to seam about, moving to the off-side or leg-side. If the captain has no 'seamers' in his side and the opposition have, then he will opt to field, to prevent the opposition from taking advantage of the conditions.

Alternatively, if a team is strong on batting but weak on bowling, he may choose to field first, in the belief that the best way of winning is to chase runs.

Although there are many factors that will influence his decision whether to bat or field first, it is the ability and experience of the captain to assess these factors that is the most significant.

The fielding captain

You have made the decision as captain to field. Now you must take the field with a winning tactical plan. You have to outline these tactics to your side, so that they are prepared. These tactics will probably have to be varied in response to conditions during the game. If the game is slipping away and there is a chance of defeat, then your objective will become to play for a draw.

Now is the time when it will show if your team is not well drilled and alert. There is little worse, than a captain who has to remind his players constantly of their positions in the field. This very often happens when there is a left-handed and a right-handed batsman together. If the fielders are alert, this field changing need not be time consuming.

Make sure that fielders are not fielding in 'halfway positions', ie. where they are too deep to save singles and too close up to cut off fours. This decision will always be influenced by the state of the pitch. If the pitch is hard and fast, put your men deeper than if the pitch is damp and slow, in an effort to cut off the runs or take the catches.

Never over-bowl your bowlers, especially early on in an innings. It is important to recognise when a bowler is tired or losing his penetration and take him off. If the pitch is bad, then it may need only your two or three main bowlers to bowl the opposition out. Equally, if the pitch is a good batting strip, you will need to use all your options and try to make things happen. If the pitch is dull and lifeless, try the unexpected, in an attempt to break the batsman's concentration, it may result in a wicket.

The batting captain

The captain plays just as important a part while the team is batting, as he does when they are fielding. While on the field the captain's role is to be constantly in the play, but when your side is batting you must adopt the role of mathematician and adviser. You need to be constantly aware of the target to be aimed for, especially when batting second.

Always aim for a settled batting line-up with your best batsmen normally going in at 3 and 4. Having said this, ideally your numbers 1 and 2 will be stroke makers, but their role is to see the shine off the ball and be the foundation of the innings. This is vitally important when batting, to get off to a good start without losing early, cheap wickets. If this happens the rest of the batting side is under pressure and the 3 and 4 batsmen finish up being 'openers'.

The middle order, numbers 5 and 6, should be adaptable to the needs of the situation, to force the pace, or consolidate when quick wickets have fallen.

The batsmen from 7 onwards are normally the wicket-keeper and bowlers, although it goes without saying that they should be capable of scoring runs.

As captain you must make all your batsmen aware of their responsibilities. This you can do by example. When batting yourself, you should try to play the type of innings required by the situation.

Encourage the batsmen before they go out to bat, giving advice where necessary on the type of innings you want them to play. Never remonstrate with a batsman on his arrival in the dressing room when he has just been out to a bad shot. It's better to leave it until the team talk later on, and then go over the mistakes that everyone has made in the course of the game.

If, however, the batsman has totally ignored your instructions and played a rash stroke to the detriment of his side, he should be told of his error immediately, but in private.

One of the most important decisions for the batting captain is when to declare. This only comes with experience and many factors can influence this decision, such as the state of the pitch, the quality of the opposition, the time left in the match etc.

The timing of the declaration is important, as it can influence the result so much. It must be sporting enough to invite the opposition to go for the match, but not so much so that they win too easily. Allowing the opposition to go for the runs increases the chance of claiming their wickets as mistakes arise.

It is important to impress upon the members of your team, the value of running between the wickets. Not only does it keep the scoreboard 'ticking over' but also saps the confidence of the opposition.

So, to sum up the batting captain. He should always watch his team's innings with his non-batting players, at the same time, discussing the way the game is going, the need to change the order when required to suit the situation or change the course of the game. He must keep his eye on the scoreboard and work out run rates required and most of all give praise when a batsman has played a good innings for his side.

Fitness and Training

Fitness plays a great part in competitive cricket. A team that includes unfit players does not look impressive. The important thing to remember when players are training for physical fitness, is to vary the routine. To repeat the same routine day after day will only have an adverse effect. Boredom soon sets in. Also the routine should incorporate the basic techniques used in cricket. For example, running quick singles means sprinting for 22 yards at regular intervals. So one of the routines should involve short sprints. This can be done very simply.

Mark out a distance of approximately 22 yards. In turn, the players sprint between the markers, slow down as they go past, turn and slowly approach the marker, then sprint back to the start. This is repeated several times, then a short rest is allowed before starting the sequence again.

Training is made more interesting if the element of competition is introduced. When using shuttle running, the coach should divide the players into groups of equal number and incorporate relay races, group against group.

Bowlers should take part in the same training sessions as the other players, but should also seek to strengthen the parts which are vulnerable, back, groin and shoulders. This can be done using weight training but before carrying out these exercises, expert advice should be sought so that muscle damage is avoided.

Warming-up is also important to all players before a match, whether fielding or batting, especially when the weather is cold. By warming-up properly injury can be averted, particularly pulled muscles in the hamstring and back areas.

Net practice

Net practice is very important to a cricketer and should always be taken seriously. The main aim of practice is to introduce, revise or improve a particular skill, primarily in batting and bowling.

Because the aim of practice is to improve a player, it is important to have a good pitch on which to do it. So ideally the practice pitch should be prepared in the same way as a match pitch. A batsman will only learn correct techniques and the confidence which is needed to play shots, on a sound surface.

The nets should always have enough width to allow a bowler to run off the pitch after delivering the ball and enough room behind the batsman to allow a wicket-keeper to practise standing up to the stumps, to a slow or medium paced bowler.

The pitch should always be marked out correctly as for a proper match. This allows a bowler to bowl as if in a match situation. He should always bowl from the correct markings, as ignoring the crease will lead to bad habits which will be carried into matches. He should also bowl off his correct run-up.

Bowlers should concentrate just as hard at practice as in a match. This is the place to experiment and improve technique. Also if a batsman has a fault in his technique, the bowlers should concentrate hard on bowling to this weakness and help him to improve.

When in the nets, batsmen should treat practice as if playing in match conditions, ie. play themselves in, get the pace of the pitch and treat every ball with respect. Don't use the nets as 'slogging' practice.

Safety is very important in the nets, whether indoors or out. Players must concentrate and keep their eyes on the ball at all times, even if they are not bowling. It is very easy to turn and talk to somebody and be hit by the ball, when it could be avoided. Remember a cricket ball can be very dangerous, it's hard!

It helps to maintain concentration in the nets, if the numbers are limited. A maximum of six is the ideal to have in each net. This allows one batting, one padded up and four bowling. It also means that the bowlers get plenty of bowling and concentrate between deliveries, before bowling the next ball.

Equipment

Protective equipment
Protective equipment is used mostly by batsmen and wicket-keepers, although in recent years, helmets for close-in fielders have become common.

Batsmen and wicket-keepers should always wear a pair of good quality, well-fitting pads. They should be as light-weight as possible, to allow quick movement without loss of protection for the knees and shins. It is ideal if a player can provide his own pads, so that once fitted comfortably, the straps can be cut to size so that they are not flapping about, as well as looking untidy.

For further protection to the legs when facing fast bowlers, the batsman can wear a thigh pad. This is worn on the thigh, under the trousers, on the front leg as it faces down the wicket to the bowler. It is usually made of fibre-glass moulded to the shape of the leg, although it can be in the form of a foam pad. It is tied securely in position around the thigh and waist with straps.

All batsmen and wicket-keepers should wear a protective 'box'. This is either made of plastic and kept in place by a pouch in the 'jockstrap', or is a metal shield, padded round the edges and kept in place by straps tied around the waist.

It is essential that the batsman's hands are protected. The important parts are the knuckles, the thumb of the bottom hand and the back of the hands. Batting gloves come in various designs, mittens, open palm and wrap-around. The batsman should choose those that he feels most comfortable in, as long as the protection is adequate.

Wicket-keepers should select a pair of gloves that are comfortable and fit well. They should not be 'sloppy' as this may cause him to fumble the ball. He may also choose to wear a pair of 'inners'. These come in dry cotton or chamois leather which may be wetted. The popular choice nowadays is to use the dry ones as they are more comfortable and soak up any perspiration from his hands.

Helmets are now an important part of a cricketer's protective equipment. They are of the lightweight type and can be used with either side pieces, full visor or face grill. They are used by batsmen to protect them against the short pitched ball and fielders when fielding in the close catching positions.

Clothing

The most vital part of a cricketer's equipment is probably his footwear. It should be comfortable and grip the ground securely. Most players prefer to use a lightweight shoe that is properly 'spiked', although bowlers usually prefer a boot which gives extra ankle support when bowling. They should be big enough to allow the player to wear a pair of thick woollen socks. They should be checked before each game to make sure that the spikes are in good order and the laces are not likely to 'snap' during the course of the game. They should be cleaned after each use and whitened.

Trousers and shirts must be comfortable. When buying trousers, it is vitally important to remember that cricket involves bending, stretching, running etc. so if they are too tight they will restrict movement.

Shirts should be thick enough to absorb perspiration during the course of a match, especially for bowlers. Bowlers and wicket-keepers should buy shirts that have plenty of width across the shoulders because of the arm movement involved. This may mean buying a size bigger than usual.

Jumpers, which should be good quality, can be bought with or without sleeves. Bowlers may choose to wear more than one at a time to prevent getting a chill, especially after bowling. It also protects the muscles and keeps them warm. Remember, it is quite easy to pull muscles that are cold.

There are various types of hats on the market and these should be worn when the sun is proving troublesome. The popular choice of headgear at present, is the white wide-brimmed hat, but a cap with a large peak is just as effective and does look a little smarter.

Players should take a pride in their appearance, both off and on the field. If you look good, you feel good.

Bats

This is probably the most expensive part of a cricketer's equipment and there is a huge choice of manufacturers. Bats are made in heavy, light or medium weight. They will have either a long handle, for tall people or short for smaller people. The right length will prevent the batsman's hands from getting too far apart.

Remember that a heavy bat takes more lifting and could interfere with the timing of the stroke play. The ideal way to select the right weight of bat is to pick it up with the top hand. If this can be done comfortably, the weight will be about right. Once the bat is chosen, read the manufacturer's advice for the care of the bat. All bats should be 'knocked-in' properly, whether they are oil or non-oil bats. If the bat needs to be oiled, wipe a rag impregnated with linseed-oil over the blade and edges of the bat but not the splice. If the bat needs to be repaired then this should be done professionally. Remember, it is the most expensive item in the equipment so it is worth looking after.

Definition of a Match

A match is played between two teams of eleven players on each side, including the captain. The captain has to nominate his players before the toss which marks the start of the game. He can't change those nominated players without the permission of the opposing team's captain. You can however field a substitute if one of your players is ill or injured, provided the other captain agrees. Your substitute isn't allowed to bat or bowl though. An injured batsman is allowed to have a runner, though the runner must already be a nominated team member and must have gloves and pads, if the man for whom he is running is wearing them.

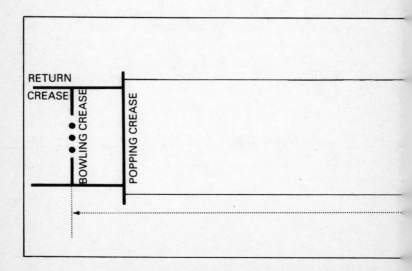

The pitch

The pitch is the area between the bowling, popping and return creases. It should be 5 ft (1.52 m.) wide, either side of a line joining the centre of the middle stumps of the wickets.

The return crease

The inside edge of the return crease marking is the crease, It is at each end of the bowling crease and at right-angles to it. It is marked to a minimum of 4 ft (1.22 m) behind the wicket and is of unlimited length. The forward extension is marked on the popping crease.

The bowling crease

The bowling crease is marked in line with the stumps at each end . It is 8ft 8 in (2.64 m) long and the stumps are in the centre.

The popping crease

The popping crease is the back edge of the crease marking, it is placed in front of and parallel to the bowling crease. The back edge of the crease marking is 4ft (1.22m) from the centre of the stumps and must extend to a minimum of 6ft (1.83 m) either side of the line of the wicket. There is no length limit.

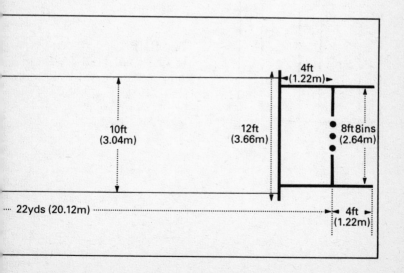

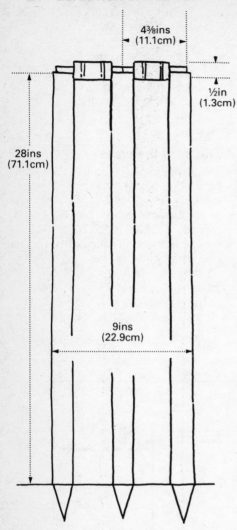

4⅜ins
(11.1cm)

½in
(1.3cm)

28ins
(71.1cm)

9ins
(22.9cm)

The wickets

There are two sets of wickets, consisting of three wooden stumps each with two sets of wooden bails on top. The wickets should be 9 ins (22.86 cm) wide.
They are pitched opposite and parallel to one another at 22 yds (20.12m) distance, between the centres of the middle two stumps.

The stumps

The stumps must show 28 ins (71.1 cm) above the ground and be of equal size. They must be big enough to stop the ball from passing between them.

The bails

The bails are 4 3/8 in (11.1cm) long and must not add more than ½ in (1.3 cm) to the height of the stumps when placed on top.

The ball

The ball must weigh not less
than 5½ oz (155.9 g) when
new, nor more than 5¾ oz
(163 g) and must be between
8³⁄₁₆ ins (22.24 cm) and 9 ins
(22.(cm) in circumference.

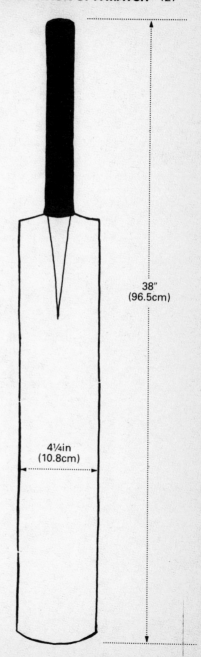

38"
(96.5cm)

4¼in
(10.8cm)

The bat

The bat must be no more
than 38 ins (96.5 cm) long
and the blade which must be
wood must be no wider than
4¼ inches (10.8 cm).